George Anson Jackson

The Apostolic Fathers

And the Apologists of the Second Century

George Anson Jackson

The Apostolic Fathers
And the Apologists of the Second Century

ISBN/EAN: 9783337404956

Printed in Europe, USA, Canada, Australia, Japan

Cover: Foto ©Lupo / pixelio.de

More available books at **www.hansebooks.com**

Early Christian Literature Primers.

Edited by Professor GEORGE P. FISHER, D. D.

THE APOSTOLIC FATHERS

AND

THE APOLOGISTS OF THE SECOND CENTURY.

BY

REV. GEORGE A. JACKSON.

NEW YORK:
D. APPLETON AND COMPANY,
549 AND 551 BROADWAY.
1879.

COPYRIGHT BY
D. APPLETON & COMPANY,
1879.

PREFACE.

IT is the design of this volume, and of the series of which it is the first, to provide intelligent persons, laymen as well as ministers, with the means of acquainting themselves, through accurate translations or summaries, with the early ecclesiastical writers. The present volume covers the interval between the close of the Apostolic Age and the last quarter of the second century. Many of the Christian writings of this period have perished altogether, sharing thus the fate which befell so large a portion of the ancient classical literature. This circumstance, however, heightens the value even of the fragments which have survived the wreck, and which serve to throw light upon the condition of the Church in the obscure opening era of its history, when doctrines began to be formulated, and the New Testament Scriptures to be collected in the Canon.

It is essential to the value of such a work that

the translations should be correctly made, and that the explanatory observations should be in accord with the latest and soundest criticism, and should be free from the influence of a theological bias. These conditions, so far as I am able to judge, have been faithfully observed by Mr. Jackson. There may be minor points on which critics may differ in judgment, and slight inaccuracies may have escaped detection; but the work will still be recognized, I trust, as fulfilling its promise, and as meeting a want which has not before been supplied.

GEORGE P. FISHER.

YALE COLLEGE, *June* 30, 1879.

CONTENTS.

INTRODUCTION: PAGE

    Patristic Literature; its value.—Period of this volume a formative one.—Divisions of the period; glimpses of its life in works of Clement and others; Christianity speaking for itself in latter part of period.—Traces of canonical and apocryphal books.—Three motives to patristic study; present incentive; aim of this volume.—List of works in Migne's Patrology 11

THE APOSTOLIC FATHERS:

Clement of Rome 23
    Epistle to the Corinthians 27
    Clementine Literature 61
Ignatius of Antioch 66
    Epistle to Polycarp 69
    Epistle to the Ephesians 72
    Epistle to the Romans 74
Polycarp of Smyrna 77
    Epistle to the Philippians 80
Barnabas 87
    Epistle 89

ASSOCIATED AUTHORS:

Hermas 100
    The Shepherd of Hermas 101
Papias 119
    Fragments 120

THE APOLOGISTS:

PAGE

Introductory Sketch.—Wide range of writings.—Two classes of apologies; Quadratus; Aristides; Epistle to Diognetus; Aristo; Agrippa Castor; Claudius Apollinaris; Miltiades; Justin; Melito; Athenagoras; Hermias; Hegesippus.—Letter of churches of Vienne and Lyons.—Heretics of the age; Basilides; Valentinus; Heraclion; Ptolemæus; Tatian; Marcion. 122

Author of Epistle to Diognetus 128
   Epistle to Diognetus 129
Justin 140
   First Apology 143
   Synopsis of Dialogue with Trypho . . . 181
Author of Muratorian Fragment 186
   Muratorian Fragment 187
Melito 189
   Extract from treatise On Faith 190
Athenagoras 192
   Chapters from the Embassy about Christians . 193
   Final Argument on the Resurrection of the Dead . 201

CHRONOLOGICAL TABLE, A.D. 1–180.

A.D.	Roman Emperors.	A.D.	Greek Writers.	A.D.	Latin Writers.	A.D.	Christian Writers.
–14	Augustus.			9	*fl.* Ovid.		
14–37	Tiberius.	18	Strabo. Apion of Alex'a.	16	*ob.* Livy.		
37–41	Caligula.			37	*fl.* Celsus, *physician*.		Scripture Writers.
41–54	Claudius.			45	*fl.* Pomponius Mela.		
54–68	Nero.			62 / 65 / 65	*ob.* Persius. / *ob.* Lucan. / *ob.* Seneca.		
68–70	Galba, Otho, Vitellius.						
70–79	Vespasian.			78	*ob.* Flaccus.		
79–81	Titus.			79	*ob.* Pliny (major).		
81–96	Domitian.			82	Juvenal.		
96–98	Nerva.						
98–117	Trajan.	99	Dion Chrysostom.	104 / 108 / 109 / 116	*ob.* Martial. / *ob.* Tacitus. / *fl.* Pliny (minor). / *fl.* Suetonius.	95 / 116	*fl.* Clement. / *ob.* Ignatius.

CHRONOLOGICAL TABLE, A.D. 1–180—(Continued).

A.D.	ROMAN EMPERORS.	A.D.	GREEK WRITERS.	A.D.	LATIN WRITERS.	A.D.	CHRISTIAN WRITERS.
117–138	Hadrian.	118 120	Epictetus. Plutarch.	117	*ob.* Quintilian.	125 135 135 135 136 136	*fl.* Barnabas. *fl.* Papias. *fl.* Hermas. Basilides, Isidorus, } heretics. Saturninus, Agrippa Castor. Quadratus. Aristo. Aristides.
138–161	Antoninus Pius.	148	Maximus of Tyre.	140	Gaius.	152 155 	Hegesippus. *ob.* Polycarp. Mar. Polycarp. *fl.* Carpocrates, Valentinus, Heracleon, } heretics. Ptolemæus, Marcion, Marcus,
161–180	Marcus Aurelius.	161 161 176 180 180	Appian. Arrian. Ptolemy. Apollonius. Pausanias. Artemidorus. Aretæus. Lucian. Marcus Aurelius.	163	*fl.* Appuleius.	165 165 168 170 170 170 176 177 178	Ep. to Diognetus. *ob.* Justin. *fl.* Tatian. *fl.* Theophilus. *fl.* Melito. Apollinaris. Muratorian fragment. *fl.* Athenagoras. Mar. Pothinus. Dionysius of Corinth. Hermias.

INTRODUCTION.

"Under the shell there was an animal, and behind the document there was a man."—TAINE.

Patristic Literature embraces the writings of the Fathers of the Ancient Church, as distinguished from the works of the Doctors of the Mediæval Church. The line between these two Christian ages can not be sharply drawn; but, speaking in a general way, the epoch of the Fathers was, in the Western Church, the first six centuries. In the Eastern Church, the patristic age may be extended to embrace John of Damascus (A. D. 750). The writers may be arranged, not unnaturally, in four groups: 1 (A. D. 95–180). The Apostolic Fathers and the Apologists, or writers contemporary with the formation of the New Testament canon. These all wrote in Greek. 2 (A. D. 180–325). The Fathers of the third century, or writers from Irenæus to the Nicene Council; partly Greek, partly Latin. 3 (A. D. 325–590). The Post-Nicene Latin Fathers. 4 (A. D. 325–750). The Post-Nicene Greek Fathers.

We study this great body of writings, not, as we study the authors of the age of Pericles, or of the age of Augustus, as models of literary form, but, as we study all ruder literatures, to find out the truths which they embody, and to discern the men standing behind the books. And yet there is much in these Christian writings which not even the polite scholar can overlook. To lose Clement of Alexandria were to lose much of our present knowledge of classical antiquity. John Chrysostom could no more be left out of the world of letters than Bossuet. The "Confessions" of Augustine is one of the few books which belong to the whole race, and will always live.

A Formative Period.—The period covered by the present volume (95–180) was essentially the formative period of the Church. At its beginning an apostle was yet living; Christianity was only fairly born into the world. At its close the Catholic Church existed, holding in her hands a defined canon of Christian Scripture. The eighty-five years intervening thus witnessed one of the most important movements in human history; and, when we reflect that almost the only knowledge we have of that movement is gained from the scanty remains of the Christian writings of the period, we shall scan the documents closely, to see the forces working behind them. Gibbon, it is well known, said: "If a man were called to fix the period in the history of the world, during which the condition of the human race was most happy and prosperous, he would, without hesitation, name that which elapsed from the death of Domitian to the accession of Commodus." It was indeed the flood-tide pause, before the civilization of the ancient world ebbed back into its ocean of oblivion. But no eye was then so practiced in reading the marks of the ages as to see in that universal lull and happiness a presage of the world's decline. Still less was there any one to note that then, at the very climax in the history of one age of the world, there was crystallizing into form a power which would scatter from the world the darkness of its impending night, and illumine the nations with a more than Antoninian brightness. No pagan could note this. Pliny, writing to Trajan of the worshipers of Christ in Bithynia, never dreamed of such a destiny for their faith. No Christian could forecast it; for none as yet regarded Christianity as a power for transforming this world, but rather as something in antagonism with the world, which latter was soon to be swept away with all its vanities and pomps. It is little wonderful, therefore, that the Christians left scanty records of their rising power; and that, just as we have to study the secular history of this age largely in its coins and architectural remains, and in the writings of its panegyrists and satirists and philosophers, so we must study its Christian history largely in the Christian writings not professedly historical that have come down to us.

Primitive Christian Life.—These writings are commonly known as those of the Apostolic Fathers and the Apologists. Speaking strictly, the Apostolic Fathers are only four in number, Clement, Ignatius, Polycarp, and Barnabas; but with these are commonly associated Hermas and Papias. Through the pages of Clement we catch glimpses of the disciples at Rome, toward the close of the first century, suffering persecution at the hands of Domitian. We see these disciples, even before the hand of persecution is withdrawn from them, taking thought for the welfare of their brethren at Corinth, where the Church is suffering from internal dissensions. The Romans, by the hand of Clement, write to the Corinthian brethren, urging submission to church authorities. Their letter contains a prayer which, it is thought, may have formed a part of the Roman liturgy. Thus we detect the beginnings of the vigorous ecclesiastical organization, and of the elaborate order of worship, which grew up in the influential church at Rome. Again, a half century later, a letter of Dionysius of Corinth shows us that the Roman Church had been contributing money to the poorer churches of Greece, and had again, by her bishop, Soter, written a letter to the Corinthians. The latter, treasuring the letter, read it on the Lord's day, as they did the former letter written them by Clement. This same Dionysius, as we learn from Eusebius, wrote various other letters to churches "for instruction in sound doctrine, for correction in discipline, for repression of heresy." To one of these letters Pinytus replied, urging Dionysius to "impart at some time more solid food, tenderly feeding the people committed to him with a letter of riper instruction, lest by continually dwelling on milk-like teaching they should insensibly grow old without advancing beyond the teaching of babes." Here we notice, as an important characteristic of this formative period, a free and filial intercommunication between the churches, and an interest both in one another's outward welfare and in a common soundness in the faith.

Again, by the epistles of Ignatius in the earlier part, and by the letter of the churches of Vienne and Lyons in the latter part of the period, we are brought to see the entire *abandon* with which the Christians gave themselves to their new faith. Martyrdom, instead of being deprecated, was often even courted as a privilege. Death by martyrdom, we must remember, was comparatively infrequent in this period. By the second quarter of the century the number of Christians, notwithstanding their social and political insignificance, must have been very great; and there was at no time anything amounting to a universal persecution. The terrible sufferings of the Christians at Vienne and Lyons, in A. D. 177, had had nothing approaching a parallel since the days of Domitian. Still there was enough of persecution to keep always alive the martyr spirit, and no conception of the growing Church of the second century is complete that does not make this spirit prominent.

Then, standing out through every epistle and apology, especially appearing in the "Shepherd of Hermas," we see evidence of the struggle for moral purity which Christians were compelled to wage amidst the corruption of paganism. To come "out from the world" was to the believer of that day no figure of speech, but the actual entrance into a new moral atmosphere. Reading the "Shepherd," and remembering that it appeared in the midst of a society differing little from that satirized by Juvenal, we no longer wonder at the esteem in which it was held by the early Christians, but we almost join with them in calling it an inspired book.

Nor must we forget, in our estimate of these early believers, that many of them were characterized by a certain crudeness of conception, not to say credulity and narrowness, such as would to-day seem strange in any one but a child. The epistle of Barnabas illustrates this feature, and, more strikingly, fragments from Papias's "Oracles of the Lord." The latter writer held to the grossest of chiliastic or millennial ideas; and yet he doubtless represented a large element in the growing Christian community.

As the period advances, we find that Christianity is becoming more and more conscious of its own existence and importance in the great world. Whereas the earlier Christian writings were simply letters or writings from one to another among themselves, before the middle of the century Christian works come to be addressed to others outside the body of believers. The latter part of the period therefore is known as the "Age of the Apologists," which name implies that the new society was no longer wholly unknown; that it had found its voice, and was speaking for itself. Reaching at first only the humble and unlearned ranks of society, the new faith had in it that which appealed powerfully to the philosophic mind. Mere sophists, of course, despised it; but the true lovers of wisdom began to see in it a diviner philosophy than that of the Academy or the Porch. Not a few among them embraced Christianity, and became its most zealous defenders and propagators, often retaining in their new calling the philosopher's cloak which they had worn before conversion. The services of these philosophers were of two kinds. They were evangelists—"men inspired with godly zeal to copy the pattern of the apostles," says Eusebius—teaching Christian doctrine by word of mouth in all the centers of learning. They were also writers, preparing treatises in exposition and defense of the faith. Such explanatory and apologetic writings make up the larger and the characteristic part of the later Christian works of the period.

The New Testament Canon.—Again, besides these glimpses of the primitive life of the Church, we get other information of value from the early literature. The New Testament canon was then forming, and from time to time throughout the period we catch sight of the several New Testament books in the hands of our authors, and treated by them as Scripture. At the close of the period we find in existence the Muratorian Fragment, which gives us almost our complete New Testament.

But side by side with these traces of our received books of Scripture, we see in the hands of Christians of the second century certain *apocryphal* writings. These works are of two kinds: 1. Works claiming apostolic authority; 2. Works making no claim to inspiration, but only to embody traditions which had been handed down concerning our Lord or his apostles. Of the first class, which were few in number, and principally modifications of our canonical books, only those mentioned in connection with Basilides, Valentinus, and Marcion can claim our attention in this period. The second class of apocryphal works, which related chiefly the history of Joseph and Mary, the infancy of Jesus, and the acts of Pilate, came in time to be numerous. None of them, in their present form, belonged to the second century; but many of the traditions which they embody existed thus early, and perhaps portions of the "Protevangelion of James," of the "Acts of Pilate," and of the "Gospel of Thomas," then existed in written form.

Patristic Studies.—A thought should be bestowed upon the history of patristic studies. Speaking in a general way, there have been three several incentives to an examination of the works of the Fathers, particularly the earlier writings. The first of these grew out of the Protestant Reformation. Luther, Calvin, Melanchthon, and the other leading Reformers studied the patristic writers, especially Augustine. The Catholic Church, claiming that the early writers were upon her side, in the hundred years or more after the Council of Trent, produced many learned scholars in this department, most of whom studied and wrote in the interests of their church. On the other hand, Protestants, looking to Scripture alone as authoritative, made less of the early ecclesiastical writers, and, outside the Church of England, studied them with a less sympathetic spirit. Patristic studies thus received a powerful impulse from a desire on the part of Catholic writers to uphold the peculiar theological and ecclesiastical views of their church.

The Church of England held an exceptional position among Protestants. Her members, as distinguished from non-episcopal reformers, retained a very high regard for the primitive Fathers; and among them arose many learned and enthusiastic patristic scholars. The earlier of these, going further in this respect than the Catholics, who allowed for a development of doctrines, stoutly claimed that the opinions and practices of their church were substantially identical with those of the Church in the first centuries. The spirit animating these earlier Anglican scholars was thus a spirit of loyalty to the Church of England.

The third interest in which patristic study has been undertaken, the controlling one to-day, is that of a broad Christian scholarship, irrespective of the defense or overthrow of particular views. Formerly two branches of the Church enjoyed a kind of monopoly of this department of Christian learning; but now, influenced by this broader motive, the whole Church has entered the field, and Lutheran and Puritan, alike with Romanist and Anglican, desire to know who the Fathers were and what they wrote. Writings upon the earlier Christian works, so far as they are controversial, are now directed, not against peculiar views within the Church, but against outside attacks upon Christianity itself. But, happily, most readers of Christian literature have other than controversial ends in view. Happily, too, men are better able than they once were to see valuable Christian truths in non-theological forms, or in forms differing widely from their own ways of expressing the same truths. Classes, therefore, who have in former times turned away from the early writers because they did not present systematic schemes of the plan of salvation, or because, judged by certain standards, they seemed sometimes to incline to heresy, are now glad to pick out the spiritual gems lying in these old mines.

Aim of this Work.—It is in recognition of this broad interest of Christians of every name that this series has been undertaken. Few clergymen, even, have opportunities to make extended studies in this field; yet at a day when "Supernatural Religion" is still fresh in men's minds, and when the historical foundations of Christianity are freely discussed in periodical literature, not only every clergyman but every reader needs to know something of Clement, and Ignatius, and Polycarp, and Justin—at least who they were, what works they wrote, and when they wrote them. Such information this volume attempts to give. By comparing the contents of the book with the list of works in Migne's "Patrology," it will be seen that we are able to embrace in this small compass a large part of the genuine extant writings of the Apostolic Fathers and the Apologists. If, by his efforts, the main results of modern critical study of the Fathers are made generally accessible, the aim of the author will be reached. G. A. J.

The following are the works of the Apostolic Fathers, the Apologists, and contemporaneous ecclesiastical writers to the time of Irenæus, as given in Migne's "Patrology." All that are now generally allowed to be genuine are printed in italics. Those given entire in this volume are marked with a star. Those of which extracts or summaries are given are marked with a dagger.

CLEMENT:
    * *Epistle to the Corinthians*, I.; Epistle to the Corinthians, II.; Two Epistles to Virgins.
    The Apostolical Constitutions; Recognitions of Clement. Clementine Homilies; Epitome of the Acts of Peter; Liturgy of Clement.

BARNABAS:
    † *The Catholic Epistle*. (Not, however, Barnabas the Apostle.)

INTRODUCTION.

St. Matthew the Apostle:
  Fragments.

St. Bartholomew the Apostle:
  Brief Sentence.

Pope Anacletus:
  Epistles and Decrees.

St. Hermas:
  † *The Shepherd of Hermas.*

Anonymous:
  Testament of the Twelve Patriarchs.

Anonymous:
  * *Epistle to Diognetus.* (Unquestionably very ancient, and so marked like the genuine epistles.)

Presbyters and Deacons of Achaia:
  Epistle concerning the Martyrdom of St. Andrew.

St. Dionysius the Areopagite:
  The Celestial Hierarchy; Of the Ecclesiastical Hierarchy; Treatise on the Divine Names; Of Mystical Theology; Ten Epistles; Liturgy of St. Dionysius. (These works were written not earlier than the fourth, probably in the fifth, century.)

St. Ignatius the Martyr:
  * *Genuine Epistles* (Vossian; the Curetonian given here). Seven interpolated Epistles; eight spurious Epistles; Liturgy of St. Ignatius.
  —The Martyrdom of St. Ignatius.

St. Polycarp:
  * *Epistle to the Philippians;* Fragments.
  —Letter of the Church at Smyrna concerning the Martyrdom of Polycarp. (A very early document, but its *authenticity* is questioned, as also the *genuineness* of portions of it.)

Popes Evaristus, Alexander I., Sixtus I., Telesphorus, Hyginus, Pius I., Eleutherus:
  Epistles and Decrees.

St. Melito:
  † *Fragments.*

St. Papias:
  † *Fragments from "Oracles of the Lord."*

St. Quadratus:
  Fragments from Apology.

ARISTO PELLÆUS, ST. CLAUDIUS APOLLINARIS, ST. HEGESIPPUS PANTÆNUS, RHODON:
Fragments.

MAXIMUS, BISHOP OF JERUSALEM:
Fragment from book " De Materia."

POLYCRATES, BISHOP OF EPHESUS:
Fragment from Letter to Victor; Acts of St. Timothy.

ST. THEOPHILUS, BISHOP OF CÆSAREA:
Fragment from Epistle on the Paschal Question.

ST. SERAPION, BISHOP OF ANTIOCH, APOLLONIUS:
Fragments.

ANONYMOUS:
Epistle of the Churches at Vienne and Lyons on the Martyrdom of Pothinus and others; Fragment.

ST. VICTOR, POPE:
Epistles.

ARCHÆUS, AN AFRICAN BISHOP:
Fragment.

ST. JUSTIN (MARTYR):
Address to the Greeks; Hortatory Address to the Greeks; On the Sole Government of God.
† *Apology* I.
Apology II.
† *Dialogue with Trypho.*

TATIAN:
Address to the Greeks.

ATHENAGORAS:
† *A Mission about Christians.*
† *On the Resurrection of the Dead.*

ST. THEOPHILUS, BISHOP OF ANTIOCH:
Three Books to Autolycus.

HERMIAS, PHILOSOPHER:
A Deriding of the Gentile Philosophers.

THE APOSTOLIC FATHERS.

CLEMENT OF ROME.

THE transitions of the moral world, like those of the physical, are not abrupt. Between the plane on which stood Paul and Peter and John, and the perceptibly lower plane of the writers of the second century, intervenes a terrace on which stands Clement of Rome. Our positive knowledge of this Father is small, but is sufficient to invest him with a dignity becoming a companion and successor of the two great apostles in the foremost church of the early Christian world. Around his name clustered all those vague traditions of the Roman Church which needed only the magic of an honored name to crystallize them into historic form. Upon Clement, unwilling and declining the honor—runs the tradition—Peter laid hold, and compelled him to take the bishop's chair which he was about to leave; at the same time communicating to him "the power of binding and loosing, so that with respect to everything which he shall ordain in the earth, it shall be decreed in the heavens." With this prestige it is little wonder that he was early thought of as the author of the Epistle to the Hebrews; or that Clement of Alexandria calls him the "Apostle Clement"; or that modern critics have invested him with the dignity of imperial connections. This last supposition identifies him with Flavius Clemens, who was a cousin of the Emperor Domitian and husband of Flavia Domitilla, also of imperial blood. This Flavius Clemens was colleague of Domitian in the consulship, and his children had been selected by the Emperor as successors to the throne; but upon a charge of atheism—the profession of Christianity—Domitian suddenly put him to death and banished his wife to an island. Now it appears, both from the Epistles of St. Paul and from monuments that have lately been recovered from ancient Christian burial-places, that Christianity very early gained a foothold in the imperial palace. It is moreover probable, from the absence from Clement's epistle of all personal allusions to the persecutors of the Christians, although they were at that very time suffering persecution, that he was writing, if not from Cæsar's own household, at least from one of the great households closely allied, in which he was in actual daily intercourse with the agents of the Emperor. Furthermore, there are in the epistle some indications that Clement was acquainted with Roman history and literature, and that he identifies himself with the Romans. But however pleasant the fancy, it would be presumptuous from these data to assume so princely a rank as that of Flavius Clemens for one of the earliest bishops of Rome. Other critics therefore suppose him to have been a freedman of this noble Christian, and perhaps of Jewish descent; while still others, following Origen, hold to his identity with the Clement of Phil. iv., and suppose that he was a Philippian. But, dismissing all mere conjectures as to his exact rank and condition in life, we do know that there was a Clement among the first three bishops of the Church at Rome, and that he was probably the third in order. We learn this from the mention of Clement's name in prayers of the Roman Church which date from the second century, and also from the testimony of Irenæus. We know, too, that in the reign of Domitian, Clement, in the name of the Roman Church, wrote a letter to the Corinthian Church. This we learn from the combined testimonies of Hegesippus, the first historian of the Church, and Dionysius of Corinth, both which testimonies are preserved in Eusebius. This Epistle to the Corinthians is still extant, and is universally acknowledged to be genuine. It was written about A. D. 95, and is probably the only genuine work of Clement which we have. Closely connected with this work in history is another, which bears the name of the "Second Epistle of Clement to the Corinthians," and which long passed as Clement's even among critics. Scholars now, however, agree that it can not be ascribed to the same author as the first epistle, some thinking it the work of Clement of Alexandria, some that of another Clement contemporary with Pius, the brother of Hermas. It has, moreover, the form of a homily rather than of a letter. Besides these, four other letters bear the name of Clement: two Epistles on Virginity, extant only in Syriac, which, though not genuine, are of very early date; and two Epistles to James the Lord's Brother, one of which doubtless dates from the last half of the second century.

In addition to these epistolary writings, a considerable body of Clementine literature, so called, has attached itself to our author's name. It is embodied in two works, or two recensions of the same work, known as the "Clementina" and the "Recognitiones," and in the "Apostolical Constitutions." These works will be described in the appendix to Clement's Epistle.

To speak briefly now of this genuine epistle. Until very lately only one manuscript of the work was known—the Alexandrian manuscript of the New Testament (*cir.* A. D. 450), in which the first and second Epistles to the Corinthians were recorded after the canonical books. This position confirms the testimony of Eusebius that, though not considered canonical, they were so much esteemed as to be frequently read in the churches. This Alexandrian manuscript, which has been known to scholars 250 years, was confessedly imperfect; so that when, in 1875, Bryennios published at Constantinople a new and entire manuscript, found in that city, critics hailed the event with delight. Very soon after this discovery, another (Syriac) manuscript was brought to light, thus giving us at last a substantially perfect text. The gap thus filled was great. Toward the close of the first epistle, the Alexandrian manuscript had lost about a tenth part of the whole, while of the second epistle some two fifths was wanting. The new portions give important hints as to the dates of both epistles, as to the stage of liturgical development in the Roman Church at the writing of the first epistle, and as to the homiletical rather than epistolary character of the second (so-called) epistle. Besides the larger defects of the Alexandrian manuscript, there were a number of minor chasms caused by age and use; and not the slightest advantage accruing from the discovery of the new manuscripts, at least to the non-critical world, is the confidence they give us in the learning and acumen of such critics as Lightfoot and Harnack, who had previously edited the Alexandrian text, and not a few of whose conjectural readings are now absolutely established.

For the contents of the epistle the reader is referred to the work itself. It is given entire, save some of the longer and more exact Scripture quotations, in making which the author must have had the Septuagint version before him. The translation is Lightfoot's, and is the only translation from the Greek used in this volume in which emendations from a critical text have not been necessary.

The reader should carefully note the resemblance, both in thought and in forms of expression, to the New Testament epistles, especially the Epistle to the Hebrews.

THE EPISTLE OF CLEMENT TO THE CORINTHIANS.

The church of God which sojourneth in Rome to the church of God which sojourneth in Corinth, to them which are called and sanctified by the will of God through our Lord Jesus Christ. Grace to you and peace from Almighty God through Jesus Christ be multiplied.

1. By reason of the sudden and repeated calamities and reverses which are befalling us, brethren,

we consider that we have been somewhat tardy in giving heed to the matters of dispute that have arisen among you, dearly beloved, and to the detestable and unholy sedition so alien and strange to the elect of God, which a few headstrong and self-willed persons have kindled to such a pitch of madness, that your name, once revered and renowned, and lovely in the sight of all men, hath been greatly reviled. For who that had sojourned among you did not approve your most virtuous and steadfast faith? Who did not admire your sober and forbearing piety in Christ? Who did not publish abroad your magnificent disposition of hospitality? Who did not congratulate you on your perfect and sound knowledge? For ye did all things without respect of persons, and ye walked after the ordinances of God, submitting yourselves to your rulers, and rendering to the older men among you the honor which is their due. On the young, too, ye enjoined modest and seemly thoughts; and the women ye charged to perform all their duties in a blameless and seemly and pure conscience, cherishing their own husbands, as is meet; and ye taught them to keep in the rule of obedience, and to manage the affairs of their household in seemliness, with all discretion.

2. And ye were all lowly in mind and free from arrogance, yielding rather than claiming submission, *more glad to give than to receive*, and content with the provisions which God supplieth. And giving heed unto his words, ye laid them up diligently in your hearts, and his sufferings were before your eyes. Thus a profound and rich peace was given to all, and an insatiable desire of doing good. An abundant outpouring also of the Holy Spirit fell upon all; and being full of holy counsel, in excellent zeal, and with a pious confidence, ye stretched out your hands to Almighty God, supplicating him

to be propitious, if unwittingly ye had committed any sin. Ye had conflict day and night for all the brotherhood, that the number of his elect might be saved with fearfulness and intentness of mind. Ye were sincere and simple and free from malice one toward another. Every sedition and every schism was abominable to you. Ye mourned over the transgressions of your neighbors; ye judged their shortcomings to be your own. Ye repented not of any well-doing, but were *ready unto every good work*. Being adorned with a most virtuous and honorable life, ye performed all your duties in the fear of him. The commandments and the ordinances of the Lord were *written on the tables of your hearts*.

3. All glory and enlargement was given unto you, and that was fulfilled which is written: *My beloved ate and drank and was enlarged and waxed fat and kicked*. Hence come jealousy and envy, strife and sedition, persecution and tumult, war and captivity. So men were stirred up, *the mean against the honorable*, the ill reputed against the highly reputed, the foolish against the wise, the young *against the elder*. For this cause *righteousness* and peace *stand aloof*, while each man hath forsaken the fear of the Lord and become purblind in the faith of him, neither walketh in the ordinances of his commandments, nor liveth according to that which becometh Christ, but each goeth after the lusts of his evil heart, seeing that they have conceived an unrighteous and ungodly jealousy, through which also *death entered into the world*.

4. For so it is written: *And it came to pass after certain days that Cain brought of the fruits of the earth a sacrifice unto God, and Abel he also brought of the firstlings of the sheep and of their fatness. And God looked upon Abel and upon his gifts, but unto Cain and unto his sacrifices he gave no heed. And Cain sorrowed exceedingly, and his countenance fell. And God*

said unto Cain, Wherefore art thou very sorrowful? and wherefore did thy countenance fall? If thou hast offered aright and hast not divided aright, didst thou not sin? Hold thy peace. Unto thee shall he turn, and thou shalt rule over him. And Cain said to Abel his brother, Let us go over unto the plain. And it came to pass, while they were in the plain, that Cain rose up against Abel his brother and slew him. Ye see, brethren, jealousy and envy wrought a brother's murder. By reason of jealousy our father Jacob ran away from the face of Esau his brother. Jealousy caused Joseph to be persecuted even unto death, and to come even to bondage. Jealousy compelled Moses to flee from the face of Pharaoh, king of Egypt, while it was said to him by his own countrymen, *Who made thee a judge or a decider over us? Wouldest thou slay me, even as yesterday thou slewest the Egyptian?* By reason of jealousy Aaron and Miriam were lodged outside the camp. Jealousy brought Dathan and Abiram down alive to Hades, because they made sedition against Moses, the servant of God. By reason of jealousy David was not only envied by aliens, but was persecuted also by Saul, king of Israel.

5. But, to pass from the examples of ancient days, let us come to those champions who lived nearest to our time. Let us set before us the noble examples which belong to our generation. By reason of jealousy and envy the greatest and most righteous pillars of the church were persecuted, and contended even unto death. Let us set before our eyes the good apostles. There was Peter, who by reason of unrighteous jealousy endured not one nor two but many labors, and thus having borne his testimony went to his appointed place of glory. By reason of jealousy and strife Paul by his example pointed out the prize of patient endurance. After that he had been seven times in bonds, had been

driven into exile, had been stoned, had preached in the East and in the West, he won the noble renown which was the reward of his faith, having taught righteousness unto the whole world, and having reached the farthest bounds of the West; and when he had borne his testimony before the rulers, so he departed from the world and went unto the holy place, having been found a notable pattern of patient endurance.

6. Unto these men of holy lives was gathered a vast multitude of the elect, who through many indignities and tortures, being the victims of jealousy, set a brave example among ourselves. By reason of jealousy matrons and maidens and slave-girls being persecuted, after they had suffered cruel and unholy insults, safely reached the goal in the race of faith, and received a noble reward, feeble though they were in body. Jealousy hath estranged wives from their husbands, and changed the saying of our father Adam, *This now is bone of my bones and flesh of my flesh.* Jealousy and strife have overthrown great cities and uprooted great nations.

7. These things, dearly beloved, we write, not only as admonishing you, but also as putting ourselves in remembrance. For we are in the same lists, and the same contest awaiteth us. Wherefore let us forsake idle and vain thoughts; and let us conform to the glorious and venerable rule which hath been handed down to us; and let us see what is good and what is pleasant and what is acceptable in the sight of him that made us. Let us fix our eyes on the blood of Christ and understand how precious it is unto his Father, because being shed for our salvation it won for the whole world the grace of repentance. Let us review all the generations in turn, and learn how from generation to generation the Master hath given a place for repentance unto them that desire to turn to him.

Noah preached repentance, and they that obeyed were saved. Jonah preached destruction unto the men of Nineveh; but they, repenting of their sins, obtained pardon of God by their supplications and received salvation, albeit they were aliens from God.

8. The ministers of the grace of God through the Holy Spirit spake concerning repentance. Yea, and the Master of the universe himself spake concerning repentance with an oath: *For as I live, saith the Lord, I desire not the death of the sinner, so much as his repentance;* and he added also a merciful judgment: *Repent ye, O house of Israel, of your iniquity; say unto the sons of my people, Though your sins reach from the earth even unto the heaven, and though they be redder than scarlet and blacker than sackcloth, and ye turn unto me with your whole heart and say, Father, I will give ear unto you as unto an holy people.* And in another place he saith on this wise [Isa. i. 16–20, quoted very exactly]. Seeing then that he desireth all his beloved to be partakers of repentance, he confirmed it by an act of his almighty will.

9. Wherefore let us be obedient unto his excellent and glorious will; and presenting ourselves as suppliants of his mercy and goodness, let us fall down before him and betake ourselves unto his compassions, forsaking the vain toil and the strife and the jealousy which leadeth unto death. Let us fix our eyes on them that ministered perfectly unto his excellent glory. Let us set before us Enoch, who being found righteous in obedience was translated, and his death was not found. Noah, being found faithful, by his ministration preached regeneration unto the world, and through him the Master saved the living creatures that entered into the ark in concord.

10. Abraham, who was called the "friend," was

found faithful in that he rendered obedience unto the words of God. He through obedience went forth from his land and from his kindred and from his father's house, that leaving a scanty land and a feeble kindred and a mean house he might inherit the promises of God. For he saith unto him, *Go forth* [quoting Gen. xii. 1-3]. And again, when he was parted from Lot, God saith unto him, *Look up* [quoting Gen. xiii. 14-16]. And again he saith: *And God led Abraham forth and said unto him, Look up unto the heaven and count the stars, and see whether thou canst count them. So shall thy seed be. And Abraham believed God, and it was reckoned unto him for righteousness.* For his faith and hospitality a son was given unto him in old age, and by obedience he offered him a sacrifice unto God on one of the mountains which he showed him.

11. For his hospitality and godliness Lot was saved from Sodom, when all the country round about was judged by fire and brimstone; the Master having thus foreshown that he forsaketh not them which set their hope on him, but appointeth unto punishment and torment them which swerve aside. For when his wife had gone forth with him, being otherwise minded and not in accord, she was appointed for a sign hereunto, so that she became a pillar of salt unto this day, that it might be known unto all men that they which are double-minded and they which doubt concerning the power of God are set for a judgment and for a token unto all the generations.

12. For her faith and hospitality Rahab the harlot was saved. [Account of Rahab's harboring and saving the spies, from Josh. ii.] And moreover they gave her a sign, that she should hang out from her house a scarlet thread, thereby showing beforehand that through the blood of the Lord there shall be redemption unto all them that believe and hope

on God. Ye see, dearly beloved, not only faith, but prophecy, is found in the woman.

13. Let us therefore be lowly minded, brethren, laying aside all arrogance and conceit and folly and anger, and let us do that which is written. For the Holy Ghost saith: *Let not the wise man boast in his wisdom, nor the strong in his strength, neither the rich in his riches; but he that boasteth let him boast in the Lord, that he may seek him out, and do judgment and righteousness;* most of all remembering the words of the Lord Jesus which he spake, teaching forbearance and long-suffering; for thus he spake: *Have mercy, that ye may receive mercy: forgive, that it may be forgiven to you. As ye do, so shall it be done to you. As ye give, so shall it be given unto you. As ye judge, so shall ye be judged. As ye show kindness, so shall kindness be shown unto you. With what measure ye mete, it shall be measured withal to you.*

14. Therefore it is right and proper, brethren, that we should be obedient unto God, rather than follow those who in arrogance and unruliness have set themselves up as leaders in abominable jealousy. For we shall bring upon us no common harm, but rather great peril, if we surrender ourselves recklessly to the purposes of men who launch out into strife and seditions, so as to estrange us from that which is right. Let us be good one toward another, according to the compassion and sweetness of him that made us. For it is written: *The good shall be dwellers in the land, and the innocent shall be left on it; but they that transgress shall be destroyed utterly from it.* And again he saith: *I saw the ungodly lifted up on high and exalted as the cedars of Lebanon. And I passed by and behold he was not; and I sought out his place and I found it not. Keep innocence and behold righteousness; for there is a remnant for the peaceful man.*

15. Therefore let us cleave unto them that prac-

tice peace with godliness, and not unto them that desire peace with dissimulation. For he saith in a certain place: *This people honoreth me with their lips, but their heart is far from me;* and again: *They blessed with their mouth, but they cursed with their heart.* And again he saith: *They loved him with their mouth, and with their tongue they lied unto him; and their heart was not upright with him, neither were they steadfast in his covenant.* For this cause, *Let the deceitful lips be made dumb which speak iniquity against the righteous.* And again: *May the Lord utterly destroy all the deceitful lips, the tongue that speaketh proud things, even them that say, Let us magnify our tongue; our lips are our own; who is Lord over us? For the misery of the needy and for the groaning of the poor I will now arise, saith the Lord. I will set him in safety; I will deal boldly by him.*

16. For Christ is with them that are lowly of mind, not with them that exalt themselves over the flock. The scepter of the majesty of God, even our Lord Jesus Christ, came not in the pomp of arrogance or of pride, though he might have done so, but in lowliness of mind, according as the Holy Spirit spake concerning him. For he saith [quoting the whole of Isa. liii.; also Ps. xxii. 6–8]. Ye see, dearly beloved, what is the pattern that hath been given unto us; for, if the Lord was thus lowly of mind, what should we do, who through him have been brought under the yoke of his grace?

17. Let us be imitators also of them which went about in goat-skins and sheep-skins, preaching the coming of Christ. We mean Elijah and Elisha, and likewise Ezekiel, the prophets, and besides them those men also that obtained a good report. Abraham obtained an exceeding good report, and was called the friend of God; and looking steadfastly on the glory of God, he saith in lowliness of mind, *But I am dust and ashes.* Moreover, con-

cerning Job also it is thus written: *And Job was righteous and unblamable, one that was true and honored God and abstained from all evil.* Yet he accuseth himself, saying, *No man is clean from filth; no, not though his life be but for a day.* Moses was called *faithful in all his house*, and through his ministration God judged Egypt with the plagues and the torments which befell them. Howbeit he also, though greatly glorified, yet spake no proud words, but said when an oracle was given to him at the bush, *Who am I, that thou sendest me? Nay, I am feeble of speech and slow of tongue.* And again he saith, *But I am smoke from the pot.*

18. But what must we say of David, that obtained a good report? of whom God said, *I have found a man after my heart, David the son of Jesse: with eternal mercy have I anointed him.* Yet he too saith unto God: *Have mercy* [quoting Ps. li. 1–17].

19. The humility, therefore, and the submissiveness of so many and so great men, who have thus obtained a good report, hath through obedience made better not only us, but also the generations which were before us, even them that received his oracles in fear and truth. Seeing then that we have been partakers of many great and glorious doings, let us hasten to return unto the goal of peace which hath been handed down to us from the beginning, and let us look steadfastly unto the Father and Maker of the whole world, and cleave unto his splendid and excellent gifts of peace and benefits. Let us behold him in our mind, and let us look with the eyes of our soul unto his long-suffering will. Let us note how free from anger he is toward all his creatures.

20. The heavens are moved by his direction and obey him in peace. Day and night accomplish the course assigned to them by him, without hindrance one to another. The sun and the moon

and the dancing stars according to his appointment circle in harmony within the bounds assigned to them, without any swerving aside. The earth, bearing fruit in fulfillment of his will at her proper seasons, putteth forth the food that supplieth abundantly both men and beasts and all living things which are thereupon, making no dissension, neither altering anything which he hath decreed. Moreover, the inscrutable depths of the abysses and the unutterable statutes of the nether regions are constrained by the same ordinances. The basin of the boundless sea, gathered together by his workmanship into its reservoirs, passeth not the barriers wherewith it is surrounded; but even as he ordered it, so it doeth. For he said, *So far shalt thou come, and thy waves shall be broken within thee.* The ocean which is impassable for men, and the worlds beyond it, are directed by the same ordinances of the Master. The seasons of spring and summer and autumn and winter give way in succession to one another in peace. The winds in their several quarters at their proper season fulfill their ministry without disturbance; and the ever-flowing fountains, created for enjoyment and health, without fail give their breasts which sustain the life of men. Yea, the smallest of living things come together in concord and peace. All these things the great Creator and Master of the universe ordered to be in peace and concord, doing good unto all things, but far beyond the rest unto us who have taken refuge in his compassionate mercies through our Lord Jesus Christ, to whom be the glory and the majesty for ever and ever. Amen.

21. Look ye, brethren, lest his benefits, which are many, turn unto judgment to all of us, if we walk not worthily of him, and do those things which are good and well pleasing in his sight with concord. For he saith in a certain place, *The Spirit of the Lord*

is a lamp searching the closets of the belly. Let us see how near he is, and how that nothing escapeth him of our thoughts or our devices which we make. It is right, therefore, that we should not be deserters from his will. Let us rather give offense to foolish and senseless men who exalt themselves and boast in the arrogance of their words, than to God. Let us fear the Lord Jesus, whose blood was given for us. Let us reverence our rulers; let us honor our elders; let us instruct our young men in the lesson of the fear of God. Let us guide our women toward that which is good; let them show forth their lovely disposition of purity; let them prove their sincere affection of gentleness; let them make manifest the moderation of their tongue through silence; let them show their love, not in factious preferences, but without partiality toward all them that fear God, in holiness. Let our children be partakers of the instruction which is in Christ; let them learn how lowliness of mind prevaileth with God, what power chaste love hath with God, how the fear of him is good and great, and saveth all them that walk therein in a pure mind with holiness. For he is the searcher out of the intents and desires; whose breath is in us, and when he listeth he shall take it away.

22. Now all these things the faith which is in Christ confirmeth: for he himself through the Holy Spirit thus inviteth us: *Come* [quoting Ps. xxiv. 11-17, 18; also Ps. xxxii. 10].

23. The Father, who is pitiful in all things, and ready to do good, hath compassion on them that fear him, and kindly and lovingly bestoweth his favors on them that draw nigh unto him with a single mind. Wherefore let us not be double-minded, neither let our soul indulge in idle humors respecting his exceeding and glorious gifts. Let this scripture be far from us where he saith: *Wretched are*

the double-minded, which doubt in their soul and say, These things we did hear in the days of our fathers also, and behold we have grown old, and none of these things hath befallen us. Ye fools, compare yourselves unto a tree; take a vine. First it sheddeth its leaves, then a shoot cometh, then a leaf, then a flower, and after these a sour berry, then a full ripe grape.* Ye see that in a little time the fruit of the tree attaineth unto mellowness. Of a truth quickly and suddenly shall his will be accomplished, the scripture also bearing witness to it, saying: *He shall come quickly and shall not tarry; and the Lord shall come suddenly into his temple, even the Holy One, whom ye expect.*

24. Let us understand, dearly beloved, how the Master continually showeth unto us the resurrection that shall be hereafter; whereof he made the Lord Jesus Christ the first fruit, when he raised him from the dead. Let us behold, dearly beloved, the resurrection which happeneth at its proper season. Day and night show unto us the resurrection. The night falleth asleep, and the day ariseth; the day departeth, and night cometh on. Let us mark the fruits, how and in what manner the sowing taketh place. *The sower goeth forth* and casteth into the earth each of the seeds; and these, falling into the earth dry and bare, decay: then out of their decay the mightiness of the Master's providence raiseth them up, and from being one they increase manifold and bear fruit.

25. Let us consider the marvelous sign which is seen in the regions of the east, that is, in the parts about Arabia. There is a bird which is named the phœnix. This, being the only one of its kind, liveth for five hundred years; and when it hath now reached the time of its dissolution that it should die, it maketh for itself a coffin of frankincense and

---

* Conjectured to be from the lost apocryphal book "Eldad and Modad," or from the "Assumption of Moses."

myrrh and the other spices, into the which in the fullness of time it entereth, and so it dieth. But as the flesh rotteth, a certain worm is engendered, which is nurtured from the moisture of the dead creature and putteth forth wings. Then, when it is grown lusty, it taketh up that coffin where are the bones of its parent, and carrying them journeyeth from the country of Arabia even unto Egypt, to the place called the City of the Sun; and in the daytime, in the sight of all, flying to the altar of the Sun, it layeth them thereupon; and this done, it setteth forth to return. So the priests examine the registers of the times, and they find that it hath come when the five hundredth year is completed.

26. Do we then think it to be a great and marvelous thing if the Creator of the universe shall bring about the resurrection of them that have served him with holiness in the assurance of a good faith, seeing that he showeth to us even by a bird the magnificence of his promise? For he saith in a certain place: *And thou shalt raise me up, and I will praise thee; and I went to rest and slept, and I was awaked, for thou art with me.* And again Job saith: *And thou shalt raise this my flesh which hath endured all these things.*

27. With this hope therefore let our souls be bound unto him that is faithful in his promises and that is righteous in his judgments. He that commanded not to lie, much more shall he himself not lie; for nothing is impossible with God save to lie. Therefore let our faith in him be kindled within us, and let us understand that all things are nigh unto him. By a word of his majesty he compacted the universe, and by a word he can destroy it. *Who shall say unto him, What hast thou done? or who shall resist the might of his strength?* When he listeth and as he listeth, he will do all things; and nothing shall pass away of those things that he hath

decreed. All things are in his sight, and nothing escapeth his counsel, seeing that *the heavens declare the glory of God and the firmament proclaimeth his handiwork. Day uttereth word unto day, and night proclaimeth knowledge unto night; and there are neither words nor speeches, whose voices are not heard.*

28. Since therefore all things are seen and heard, let us fear him and forsake the abominable lusts of evil works, that we may be shielded by his mercy from the coming judgments. For where can any of us escape from his strong hand? And what world will receive any of them that desert from his service? For the holy writing saith in a certain part: *Where shall I go, and where shall I be hidden from thy face? If I ascend into the heaven, thou art there; if I depart into the farthest parts of the earth, there is thy right hand; if I make my bed in the depths, there is thy Spirit.* Whither then shall one depart, or where shall one flee, from him that embraceth the universe?

29. Let us therefore approach him in holiness of soul, lifting up pure and undefiled hands unto him, with love toward our gentle and compassionate Father, who made us an elect portion unto himself. For thus it is written: *When* [quoting Deut. xxxii. 8, 9]. And in another place he saith: *Behold, the Lord taketh for himself a nation out of the midst of the nations, as a man taketh the first fruits of his threshing floor; and the holy of holies shall come forth from that nation.*

30. Seeing then that we are the special portion of a holy God, let us do all things that pertain unto holiness, forsaking evil speakings, abominable and impure embraces, drunkennesses and tumults, and hateful lusts, abominable adultery, hateful pride; *for God*, he saith, *resisteth the proud, but giveth grace to the lowly.* Let us therefore cleave unto those to whom grace is given from God. Let us clothe our-

selves in concord, being lowly-minded and temperate, holding ourselves aloof from all backbiting and evil speaking, being justified by works and not by words. For he saith: *He that saith much shall hear also again. Doth the ready talker think to be righteous? Blessed is the offspring of a woman that liveth but a short time. Be not thou abundant in words.** Let our praise be with God, and not of ourselves; for God hateth them that praise themselves. Let the testimony to our well-doing be given by others, as it was given unto our fathers who were righteous. Boldness and arrogance and daring are for them that are accursed of God; but forbearance and humility and gentleness are with them that are blessed of God

31. Let us, therefore, cleave unto his blessing, and let us see what are the ways of blessing. Let us study the records of the things that have happened from the beginning. Wherefore was our father Abraham blessed? Was it not because he wrought righteousness and truth through faith? Isaac with confidence, as knowing the future, was led a willing sacrifice. Jacob with humility departed from his land because of his brother, and went unto Laban and served; and the twelve tribes of Israel were given unto him.

32. If any man will consider them one by one in sincerity, he shall understand the magnificence of the gifts that are given by Him. For of Jacob are all the priests and Levites who minister unto the altar of God; of him is the Lord Jesus as concerning the flesh; of him are kings and rulers and governors in the line of Judah; yea, and the rest of his tribes are held in no small honor, seeing that God promised, saying, *Thy seed shall be as the stars of heaven.* They all, therefore, were glorified and magnified, not through themselves or their own

---

* The Septuagint rendering of Job xi. 2, 3.

works or the righteous doing which they wrought, but through his will. And so we, having been called through his will in Christ Jesus, are not justified through ourselves or through our own wisdom or understanding or piety or works which we wrought in holiness of heart, but through faith whereby the Almighty God justified all men that have been from the beginning; to whom be the glory for ever and ever. Amen.

33. What then must we do, brethren? Must we idly abstain from doing good, and forsake love? May the Master never allow this to befall us at least; but let us hasten with instancy and zeal to accomplish every good work. For the Creator and Master of the universe himself rejoiceth in his works. For by his exceeding great might he established the heavens, and in his incomprehensible wisdom he set them in order. And the earth he separated from the water that surroundeth it, and he set it firm on the sure foundation of his own will; and the living creatures which walk upon it he commanded to exist by his ordinance. Having before created the sea and the living creatures therein, he inclosed it by his own power. Above all, as the most excellent and exceeding great work of his intelligence, with his sacred and faultless hands he formed man in the impress of his own image. For thus saith God: *Let us make man after our image and after our likeness. And God made man; male and female made he them.* So, having finished all these things, he praised them and blessed them and said, *Increase and multiply.* We have seen that all the righteous were adorned in good works. Yea, and the Lord himself having adorned himself with good works rejoiced. Seeing then that we have this pattern, let us conform ourselves with all diligence to his will; let us with all our strength work the work of righteousness.

34. The good workman receiveth the bread of his work with boldness, but the slothful and careless dareth not look his employer in the face. It is, therefore, needful that we should be zealous unto well-doing, for of him are all things; since he forewarneth us, saying, *Behold the Lord, and his reward is before his face, to recompense each man according to his work.* He exhorteth us, therefore, to believe on him with our whole heart, and to be not idle nor careless unto every good work. Let our boast and our confidence be in him; let us submit ourselves to his will; let us mark the whole host of his angels, how they stand by and minister unto his will. For the scripture saith: *Ten thousands of ten thousands stood by him, and thousands of thousands ministered unto him; and they cried aloud, Holy, holy, holy is the Lord of Sabaoth; all creation is full of his glory.* Yea, and let us ourselves then, being gathered together in concord with intentness of heart, cry unto him as from one mouth earnestly that we may be made partakers of his great and glorious promises. For he saith, *Eye hath not seen and ear hath not heard, and it hath not entered into the heart of man, what great things he hath prepared for them that patiently await him.*

35. How blessed and marvelous are the gifts of God, dearly beloved! Life in immortality, splendor in righteousness, truth in boldness, faith in confidence, temperance in sanctification! And all these things fall under our apprehension. What then, think ye, are the things preparing for them that patiently await him? The Creator and Father of the ages, the All-holy One himself, knoweth their number and their beauty. Let us therefore contend, that we may be found in the number of those that patiently await him, to the end that we may be partakers of his promised gifts. But how shall this be, dearly beloved? If our mind be fixed through

faith toward God; if we seek out those things which are well pleasing and acceptable unto him; if we accomplish such things as beseem his faultless will, and follow the way of truth, casting off from ourselves all unrighteousness and iniquity, covetousness, strifes, malignities and deceits, whisperings and backbitings, hatred of God, pride and arrogance, vainglory and inhospitality. For they that do these things are hateful to God; and not only they that do them, but they also that consent unto them. For the scripture saith: *But unto* [quoting Ps. l. 16–23].

·36. This is the way, dearly beloved, wherein we found our salvation, even Jesus Christ the High Priest of our offerings, the Guardian and Helper of our weakness. Through him let us look steadfastly unto the heights of the heavens; through him we behold as in a mirror his faultless and most excellent visage; through him the eyes of our hearts were opened; through him our foolish and darkened mind springeth up unto the light; through him the Master willed that we should taste of immortal knowledge; *who being the brightness of his majesty is so much greater than angels as he hath inherited a more excellent name.* For so it is written: *Who maketh his angels spirits and his ministers a flame of fire;* but of his Son the Master saith thus: *Thou art my Son, I this day have begotten thee. Ask but of me, and I will give thee the gentiles for thine inheritance and the ends of the earth for thy possession.* And again he saith unto him: *Sit thou on my right hand, until I make thine enemies a footstool for thy feet.* Who then are these enemies? They that are wicked and resist his will.

37. Let us therefore enlist ourselves, brethren, with all earnestness in his faultless ordinances. Let us mark the soldiers that are enlisted under our rulers, how exactly, how readily, how submissively

they execute the orders given them. All are not prefects, nor rulers of thousands, nor rulers of hundreds, nor rulers of fifties, and so forth; but each man in his own rank executeth the orders given by the king and the governors. *The great without the small* can not exist, *neither the small without the great.* There is a certain mixture in all things, and therein is utility. Let us take our body as an example. The head without the feet is nothing; so likewise the feet without the head are nothing; even the smallest limbs of our body are necessary and useful for the whole body; but all members conspire and unite in subjection, that the whole body may be saved.

38. So in our case let the whole body be saved in Christ Jesus, and let each man be subject unto his neighbor, according as also he was appointed with his special grace. Let not the strong neglect the weak; and let the weak respect the strong. Let the rich minister aid to the poor; and let the poor give thanks to God, because he hath given him one through whom his wants may be supplied. Let the wise display his wisdom, not in good words, but in good works. He that is lowly in mind, let him not bear testimony to himself, but leave testimony to be borne to him by his neighbor. He that is pure in the flesh, let him be so, and not boast, knowing that it is Another who bestoweth his continence upon him. Let us consider, brethren, of what matter we were made; who and what manner of beings we were, when we came into the world; from what a sepulchre and what darkness he that molded us and created us brought us into his world, having prepared his benefits aforehand ere ever we were born. Seeing therefore that we have all these things from him, we ought in all things to give thanks to him, to whom be the glory for ever and ever. Amen.

39. Senseless and stupid and foolish and ignorant men jeer and mock at us, desiring that they themselves should be exalted in their imaginations. For what power hath a mortal? or what strength hath a child of earth? For it is written: *There* [quoting Job iv. 16 to v. 5].

40. Forasmuch then as these things are manifest beforehand, and we have searched into the depths of the divine knowledge, we ought to do all things in order, as many as the Master hath commanded us to perform at their appointed seasons. Now the offerings and ministrations he commanded to be performed with care, and not to be done rashly or in disorder, but at fixed times and seasons. And when and by whom he would have them performed he himself fixed by his supreme will: that all things being done with piety according to his good pleasure might be acceptable to his will. They therefore that make their offerings at the appointed seasons are acceptable and blessed; for while they follow the institutions of the Master they can not go wrong. For unto the high priest his proper services have been assigned, and to the priests their proper office is appointed, and upon the Levites their proper ministrations are laid. The layman is bound by the layman's ordinances.

41. Let each of you, brethren, in his own order give thanks unto God, maintaining a good conscience and not transgressing the appointed rule of his service, but acting with all seemliness. Not in every place, brethren, are the continual daily sacrifices offered, or the free-will offerings, or the sin offerings, and the trespass offerings, but in Jerusalem alone. And even there the offering is not made in every place, but before the sanctuary in the court of the altar; and this, too, through the high priest and the aforesaid ministers, after that the victim to be offered hath been inspected for blemishes. They

therefore who do anything contrary to the seemly ordinance of his will receive death as the penalty. Ye see, brethren, in proportion as greater knowledge hath been vouchsafed unto us, so much the more are we exposed to danger.

42. The apostles received the gospel for us from the Lord Jesus Christ. Jesus Christ was sent forth from God. So then Christ is from God, and the apostles are from Christ. Both therefore came of the will of God in the appointed order. Having therefore received a charge, and having been fully assured through the resurrection of our Lord Jesus Christ and confirmed in the word of God with full assurance of the Holy Ghost, they went forth with the glad tidings that the kingdom of God should come. So preaching everywhere in country and town, they appointed their first fruits, when they had proved them by the Spirit, to be bishops and deacons unto them that should believe. And this they did in no new fashion; for indeed it had been written concerning bishops and deacons from the very ancient times; for thus saith the scripture in a certain place, *I will appoint their bishops in righteousness and their deacons in faith.*

43. And what marvel, if they which were intrusted in Christ with such a work by God appointed the aforesaid persons? seeing that even the blessed Moses, who was *a faithful servant in all his house*, recorded for a sign in the sacred books all things that were enjoined upon him. And him also the rest of the prophets followed, bearing witness with him unto the laws that were ordained by him. For he, when jealousy arose concerning the priesthood, and there was dissension among the tribes which of them was adorned with the glorious name, commanded the twelve chiefs of the tribes to bring to him rods inscribed with the name of each tribe. And he took them and tied them and sealed

them with the signet rings of the chiefs of the tribes, and put them away in the tabernacle of the testimony on the table of God. And having shut the tabernacle, he sealed the keys and likewise also the doors. And he said unto them, *Brethren, the tribe whose rod shall bud, this hath God chosen to be priests and ministers unto him.* Now when morning came he called together all Israel, even the six hundred thousand men, and showed the seals to the chiefs of the tribes, and opened the tabernacle of the testimony and drew forth the rods. And the rod of Aaron was found not only with buds, but also bearing fruit. What think ye, dearly beloved? Did not Moses know beforehand that this would come to pass? Assuredly he knew it. But that disorder might not arise in Israel, he did thus, to the end that the name of the true and only God might be glorified, to whom be glory for ever and ever. Amen.

44. And our apostles knew through our Lord Jesus Christ that there would be strife over the name of the bishop's office. For this cause therefore, having received complete foreknowledge, they appointed the aforesaid persons, and afterward they provided a continuance [gave instructions] that if these should fall asleep, other approved men should succeed to their ministration. Those therefore who were appointed by them, or afterward by other men of repute with the consent of the whole church, and have ministered unblamably to the flock of Christ in lowliness of mind, peacefully and with all modesty, and for a long time have borne a good report with all—these men we consider to be unjustly thrust out from their ministration. For it will be no light sin for us, if we thrust out those who have offered the gifts of the bishop's office unblamably and holily. Blessed are those presbyters who have gone before, seeing that their departure

was fruitful and ripe; for they have no fear lest any one should remove them from their appointed place. For we see that ye have displaced certain persons, though they were living honorably from the ministration which they had kept blamelessly.

45. Be ye contentious, brethren, and jealous about the things that pertain unto salvation. Ye have searched the Scriptures, which are true, which were given through the Holy Ghost: and ye know that nothing unrighteous or counterfeit is written in them. Ye will not find that righteous persons have been thrust out by holy men. Righteous men were persecuted, but it was by the lawless; they were imprisoned, but it was by the unholy. They were stoned by transgressors; they were slain by those who had conceived a detestable and unrighteous jealousy. Suffering these things, they endured nobly. For what must we say, brethren? Was Daniel cast into the den of lions by them that feared God? Or were Ananias and Azarias and Misael shut up in the furnace of fire by them that professed the excellent and glorious worship of the Most High? Far be this from our thoughts. Who then were they that did these things? Abominable men and full of all wickedness were stirred up to such a pitch of wrath as to bring cruel suffering upon them that served God in a holy and blameless purpose, not knowing that the Most High is the champion and protector of them that in a pure conscience serve his excellent name: unto whom be the glory for ever and ever. Amen. But they that endured patiently in confidence inherited glory and honor; they were exalted, and had their names recorded by God in their memorial for ever and ever. Amen.

46. To such examples as these therefore, brethren, we also ought to cleave. For it is written: *Cleave unto the saints, for they that cleave unto them*

shall be sanctified. And again he saith in another place: *With the guiltless man thou shalt be guiltless, and with the elect thou shalt be elect, and with the crooked thou shalt deal crookedly.* Let us therefore cleave to the guiltless and righteous; and these are the elect of God. Wherefore are these strifes and wraths and factions and divisions and war among you? Have we not one God, and one Christ, and one Spirit of grace that was shed upon us? And is there not one calling in Christ? Wherefore do we tear and rend asunder the members of Christ, and stir up factions against our own body, and reach such a pitch of folly as to forget that we are members one of another? Remember the words of Jesus our Lord; for he said: *Woe unto that man. It were good for him if he had not been born, rather than that he should offend one of mine elect. It were better for him that a millstone were hanged about him, and he cast into the sea, than that he should pervert one of mine elect.* Your division hath perverted many; it hath brought many to despair, many to doubting, and all of us to sorrow. And your sedition still continueth.

47. Take up the epistle of the blessed Paul the Apostle. What wrote he first unto you in the beginning of the gospel? Of a truth he charged you in the Spirit concerning himself and Cephas and Apollos, because that even then ye had made parties. Yet that making of parties brought less sin upon you; for ye were partisans of apostles that were highly reputed, and of a man approved in their sight. But now mark ye, who they are that have perverted you and diminished the glory of your renowned love for the brotherhood. It is shameful, dearly beloved, yes, utterly shameful and unworthy of your conduct in Christ, that it should be reported that the very steadfast and ancient church of the Corinthians, for the sake of one or two per-

sons, maketh sedition against its presbyters. And this report hath reached not only us, but them also which differ from us, so that ye even heap blasphemies on the name of the Lord by reason of your folly, and moreover create peril for yourselves.

48. Let us therefore root this out quickly, and let us fall down before the Master and entreat him with tears, that he may show himself propitious and be reconciled unto us, and may restore us to the seemly and pure conduct which belongeth to our love of the brethren. For this is a gate of righteousness opened unto life, as it is written: *Open me the gates of righteousness, that I may enter in thereby and praise the Lord. This is the gate of the Lord; the righteous shall enter in thereby.* Seeing then that many gates are opened, this is that gate which is in righteousness, even that which is in Christ, whereby all are blessed that have entered in and direct their path in holiness and righteousness, performing all things without confusion. Let a man be faithful, let him be able to expound a deep saying, let him be wise in the discernment of words, let him be strenuous in deeds, let him be pure; for so much the more ought he to be lowly in mind, in proportion as he seemeth to be the greater; and he ought to seek the common advantage of all, and not his own.

49. Let him that hath love in Christ fulfill the commandments of Christ. Who can declare the bond of the love of God? Who is sufficient to tell the majesty of its beauty? The height whereunto love exalteth is unspeakable. Love joineth us unto God; love covereth a multitude of sins; love endureth all things, is long-suffering in all things. There is nothing coarse, nothing arrogant in love. Love hath no divisions; love maketh no seditions; love doeth all things in concord. In love were all the elect of God made perfect; without love no-

thing is well pleasing to God; in love the Master took us unto himself; for the love which he had toward us, Jesus Christ our Lord hath given his blood for us by the will of God, and his flesh for our flesh and his life for our lives.

50. Ye see, dearly beloved, how great and marvelous a thing is love, and there is no declaring its perfection. Who is sufficient to be found therein, save those to whom God shall vouchsafe it? Let us therefore entreat and ask of his mercy that we may be found blameless in love, standing apart from the factiousness of men. All the generations from Adam unto this day have passed away; but they that by God's grace were perfected in love dwell in the abode of the pious; and they shall be made manifest in the visitation of the kingdom of God. For it is written: *Enter into the closet for a very little while, until mine anger and my wrath shall pass away, and I will remember a good day and will raise you from your tombs.* Blessed were we, dearly beloved, if we should be doing the commandments of God in concord of love, to the end that our sins may through love be forgiven us. For it is written: *Blessed are they whose iniquities are forgiven, and whose sins are covered. Blessed is the man to whom the Lord shall impute no sin, neither is guile in his mouth.* This declaration of blessedness was pronounced upon them that have been elected by God through Jesus Christ our Lord, to whom be glory for ever and ever. Amen.

51. For all our transgressions which we have committed through any wiles of the adversary, let us entreat that we may obtain forgiveness. Yea, and they also who set themselves up as leaders of faction and division ought to look to the common ground of hope. For such as walk in fear and love desire that they themselves should fall into suffering rather than their neighbors; and they pro-

nounce condemnation against themselves rather than against the harmony which hath been handed down to us nobly and righteously. For it is good for a man to make confession of his trespasses rather than to harden his heart, as the heart of those was hardened who made sedition against Moses the servant of God; whose condemnation was clearly manifest, for they went down to hades alive, and *Death shall be their shepherd.* Pharaoh and his host and all the rulers of Egypt, *their chariots and their horsemen*, were overwhelmed in the depths of the Red Sea, and perished for none other reason but because their foolish hearts were hardened after that the signs and the wonders had been wrought in the land of Egypt by the hand of Moses the servant of God.

52. The Master, brethren, hath need of nothing at all. He desireth not anything of any man, save to confess unto him. For the elect David saith: *I will confess unto the Lord, and it shall please him more than a young calf that groweth horns and hoofs. Let the poor see it, and rejoice.* And again He saith: *Sacrifice to God a sacrifice of praise, and pay thy vows to the Most High; and call upon me in the day of thine affliction, and I will deliver thee, and thou shalt glorify me. For a sacrifice unto God is a broken spirit.*

53. For ye know, and know well, the sacred scriptures, dearly beloved, and ye have searched into the oracles of God. We write these things therefore to put you in remembrance. When Moses went up into the mountain and had spent forty days and forty nights in fasting and humiliation, God said unto him: *Moses, Moses, come down quickly hence, for my people whom thou leddest forth from the land of Egypt have wrought iniquity; they have transgressed quickly out of the way which thou didst command unto them: they have made for themselves molten images.* And the Lord said unto him: *I*

have spoken unto thee once and twice, saying, I have seen this people, and behold it is stiff-necked. Let me destroy them utterly, and I will blot out their names from under heaven, and I will make of thee a nation great and wonderful and numerous more than this. And Moses said: *Nay, not so, Lord. Forgive this people their sin, or blot me also out of the book of the living.* O mighty love! O unsurpassable perfection! The servant is bold with his Master; he asketh forgiveness for the multitude, or he demandeth that himself also be blotted out with them.

54. Who therefore is noble among you? Who is compassionate? Who is fulfilled with love? Let him say: If by reason of me there be faction and strife and divisions, I retire, I depart, whither ye will, and I do that which is ordered by the people; only let the flock of Christ be at peace with its duly appointed presbyters. He that shall have done this, shall win for himself great renown in Christ, and every place will receive him; *for the earth is the Lord's and the fullness thereof.* Thus have they done and will do that live as citizens of that kingdom of God which bringeth no regrets.

55. But, to bring forward examples of Gentiles also: Many kings and rulers, when some season of pestilence pressed upon them, being taught by oracles, have delivered themselves over to death, that they might rescue their fellow citizens through their own blood. Many have retired from their own cities, that they might have no more seditions. We know that many among ourselves have delivered themselves to bondage, that they might ransom others. Many have sold themselves to slavery, and, receiving the price paid for themselves, have fed others. Many women, being strengthened through the grace of God, have performed many manly deeds. The blessed Judith, when the city was beleaguered, asked of the elders that she might be suf-

fered to go forth into the camp of the aliens. So she exposed herself to peril and went forth for love of her country and of her people which were beleaguered; and the Lord delivered Holophernes into the hands of a woman. To no less peril did Esther also, who was perfect in faith, expose herself, that she might deliver the twelve tribes of Israel, when they were on the point to perish. For through her fasting and her humiliation she entreated the all-seeing Master, the God of the ages; and he, seeing the humility of her soul, delivered the people for whose sake she encountered the peril.

56. Therefore let us also make intercession for them that are in any transgression, that forbearance and humanity may be given them, to the end that they may yield, not unto us, but unto the will of God. For so shall the compassionate remembrance of them with God and the saints be fruitful unto them, and perfect. Let us accept chastisement, whereat no man ought to be vexed, dearly beloved. The admonition which we give one to another is good and exceeding useful; for it joineth us unto the will of God. For thus saith the holy word: *The Lord hath indeed chastened me, and hath not delivered me over unto death. For whom the Lord loveth he chasteneth, and scourgeth every son whom he receiveth. For the righteous*, it is said, *shall chasten me in mercy and shall reprove me, but let not the mercy of sinners anoint my head.* And again he saith: *Blessed* [quoting Job v. 17–26]. Ye see, dearly beloved, how great protection there is for them that are chastened by the Master; for, being a kind father, he chasteneth us to the end that we may obtain mercy through his holy chastisement.

57. Ye therefore that laid the foundation of the sedition, submit yourselves unto the presbyters and receive chastisement unto repentance, bending the knees of your heart. Learn to submit yourselves,

laying aside the arrogant and proud stubbornness of your tongue. For it is better for you to be found little in the flock of Christ and to have your name on God's roll than to be had in exceeding honor and yet be cast out from the hope of him. For thus saith the All-virtuous Wisdom: *Behold* [quoting Prov. i. 23-33].

58. Let us therefore be obedient unto his most holy and glorious name, thereby escaping the threatenings which were spoken of old by the mouth of wisdom against them which disobey, that we may dwell safely, trusting in the most holy name of his majesty. Receive our counsel, and ye shall have no occasion of regret. For as God liveth, and the Lord Jesus Christ liveth, and the Holy Spirit, who are the faith and the hope of the elect, so surely shall he, who with lowliness of mind and instant in gentleness hath without regretfulness performed the ordinances and commandments that are given by God, be enrolled and have a name among the number of them that are saved through Jesus Christ, through whom is the glory unto him for ever and ever. Amen.

59. But if certain persons should be disobedient unto the words spoken by him through us, let them understand that they will entangle themselves in no slight transgression and danger; but we shall be guiltless of this sin. And we will ask, with instancy of prayer and supplication, that the Creator of the universe may guard intact unto the end the number that hath been numbered of his elect throughout the whole world, through his beloved son Jesus Christ, through whom he called us from darkness to light, from ignorance to the full knowledge of the glory of his name.

Grant unto us, Lord, that we may set our hope on thy name, which is the primal source of all creation, and open the eyes of our hearts, that we may know thee, who alone *abidest Highest in the highest, Holy in the holy;* who *layest low the insolence of the proud;* who *scatterest the imaginings of nations;* who *settest the lowly on high,* and *bringest the lofty low;* who *makest rich and makest poor;* who *killest and makest alive;* who alone art the Benefactor of spirits and the God of all flesh; who *lookest into the abysses;* who scannest the works of man; the Succor of them that are in peril, the *Saviour of them that are in despair;* the Creator and Overseer of every spirit; who multipliest the nations upon earth, and hast chosen out from all men those that love thee through Jesus Christ, thy beloved son, through whom thou didst instruct us, didst sanctify us, didst honor us. We beseech thee, Lord and Master, to be our help and succor. Save those among us who are in tribulation; have mercy on the lowly; lift up the fallen; show thyself unto the needy; heal the ungodly; convert the wanderers of thy people; feed the hungry; release our prisoners; raise up the weak; comfort the faint-hearted. Let all the Gentiles know that *thou art God alone,* and Jesus Christ is thy son, and *we are thy people and the sheep of thy pasture.*

60. Thou through thine operations didst make manifest the everlasting fabric of the world. Thou, Lord, didst create the earth. Thou that art faithful throughout all generations, righteous in thy judgments, marvelous in strength and excellence, thou that art wise in creating and prudent in establishing that which thou hast made, that art good in the things which are seen and faithful with them that trust on thee, pitiful and compassionate, forgive us our unrighteousnesses and our transgressions and shortcomings. Lay not to our account every sin of thy servants and thine handmaids, but cleanse us with the cleansing of thy truth, and guide our steps to walk in holiness and righteousness and sin-

gleness of heart, and to do such things as are good and well pleasing in thy sight and in the sight of our rulers. Yea, Lord, make thy face to shine upon us in peace for our good, that we may be sheltered by thy mighty hand and delivered from every sin by thine uplifted arm. And deliver us from them that hate us wrongfully. Give concord and peace to us and to all that dwell on the earth, as thou gavest to our fathers, when they called on thee in faith and truth with holiness, that we may be saved, while we render obedience to thine almighty and excellent name, and to our rulers and governors upon the earth.

61. Thou, Lord and Master, hast given them the power of sovereignty through thine excellent and unspeakable might, that we, knowing the glory and honor which thou hast given them, may submit ourselves unto them, in nothing resisting thy will. Grant unto them therefore, O Lord, health, peace, concord, stability, that they may administer the government which thou hast given them without failure. For thou, O Heavenly Master, King of the ages, givest to the sons of men glory and honor and power over all things that are upon the earth. Do thou, Lord, direct their counsel according to that which is good and well pleasing in thy sight, that, administering in peace and gentleness with godliness the power which thou hast given them, they may obtain thy favor. O thou, who alone art able to do these things and things far more exceeding good than these for us, we praise thee through the High Priest and Guardian of our souls, Jesus Christ, through whom be the glory and the majesty unto thee both now and for all generations, and for ever and ever. Amen.

62. As touching those things which befit our religion and are most useful for a virtuous life to such as would guide their steps in holiness and

righteousness, we have written fully unto you, brethren. For concerning faith and repentance and genuine love and temperance and sobriety and patience we have handled every argument, putting you in remembrance that ye ought to please Almighty God in righteousness and truth and long-suffering with holiness, laying aside malice and pursuing concord in love and peace, being instant in gentleness; even as our fathers, of whom we spake before, pleased him, being lowly-minded toward their Father and God and Creator and toward all men. And we have put you in mind of these things the more gladly, since we knew that we were writing to men who are faithful and highly accounted, and have diligently searched into the oracles of the teaching of God.

63. Therefore it is right for us to give heed to so great and so many examples, and to submit the neck, and, occupying the place of obedience, to take our side with them that are the leaders of our souls, that ceasing from this foolish dissension we may attain unto the goal which lieth before us in truthfulness, keeping aloof from every fault. For ye will give us great joy and gladness, if ye render obedience unto the things written by us through the Holy Spirit, and root out the unrighteous anger of your jealousy, according to the entreaty which we have made for peace and concord in this letter. And we have also sent faithful and prudent men that have walked among us from youth unto old age unblamably, who shall also be witnesses between you and us. And this we have done that ye might know that we have had, and still have, every solicitude that ye should be speedily at peace.

64. Finally, may the All-seeing God and Master of spirits and Lord of all flesh, who chose the Lord Jesus Christ, and us through him for a peculiar people, grant unto every soul that is called after his

excellent and holy name faith, fear, peace, patience, long-suffering, temperance, chastity, and soberness, that they may be well pleasing unto his name through our High Priest and Guardian Jesus Christ, through whom unto him be glory and majesty, might and honor, both now and for ever and ever. Amen.

65. Now send ye back speedily unto us our messengers Claudius Ephebus and Valerius Bito, together with Fortunatus also, in peace and with joy, to the end that they may the more quickly report the peace and concord which is prayed for and earnestly desired by us, that we also may the more speedily rejoice over your good order.

The grace of our Lord Jesus Christ be with you and with all men in all places who have been called by God, and through him, through whom is glory and honor, power and greatness, and eternal dominion, unto him, from the ages past and for ever and ever. Amen.

CLEMENTINE LITERATURE.

Besides the letters ascribed to Clement, three works of considerable size have borrowed the sanction of his name: the "Clementine Homilies," the "Recognitions of Clement," and the "Apostolical Constitutions." The two former of these are simply two recensions of the same work, which is a religious romance embodying what purport to be discourses of the Apostle Peter. It is evidently an Ebionitic production, that is, a work of that branch of the church which retained so strong a Jewish character as to be deemed heretical by Catholic Christians. Its date is variously estimated from the middle of the second to the middle of the third century. Scholars differ as to which of the present forms was prior, and as to whether or not both were rewritten from some more primitive document. On the supposition that they were so rewritten, the original must recede very near to the earlier date named. Of the two, the "Homilies" are the more heretical, an effort having evidently been made to bring the "Recognitions" into harmony with the teachings of the church. Save in details the narrative of both the forms is the same.

THE STORY OF THE RECOGNITIONS.

Clement, a Roman citizen pondering the mysteries of life, falls into great perplexity, and determines to go to Egypt to make inquiry as to the immortality of the soul. About this time tidings come to Rome of a certain One in Judea who is preaching of the kingdom of God, and soon a disciple of His, Barnabas, appears and proclaims the Gospel, which induces Clement to set out for Judea. [The "Homilies" make Clement and Barnabas meet at Alexandria, whither Clement had been driven by adverse winds.] Coming to Cæsarea, Clement is introduced to Peter, who, under the direction of the other apostles who have just been driven from Jerusalem, has come there to oppose Simon Magus. A public discussion has been arranged; but, it being delayed for a time, Peter discourses to Clement on the preparatory Jewish dispensation, the coming and rejection of the true Prophet, and the recent history of the church. [In the "Homilies" this instruction to Clement is different, being of an esoteric nature, and declaring the text of Scripture (O. T.) to be corrupt.] The disputation with Simon lasts three days, after which Simon flies. Peter determines to follow him to the Gentile world. Having ordained Zaccheus bishop of Cæsarea, and having baptized ten thousand converts, he sets out for Tripolis, first sending before him twelve men to prepare the way. Two of the converts are Niceta and Aquila, who had been followers of Simon. Peter goes by way of Dora to Tripolis, and after preaching there three months, and baptizing many converts, he goes on toward Antioch. [The " Homilies," having given only part of the discussion, say that Simon flies to Tyre; that Clement, Niceta, and Aquila are sent thither by Peter; that Clement has a discussion with Appion on mythology; that Peter then comes by way of Tyre, Sidon, and Berytas to Tripolis.] Journeying from Tripolis, Clement relates to Peter his family history. In his youth his mother, having had a warning vision, had sailed away from Rome with his infant twin brothers, and had never been heard from afterward. His father, going in search of them, had never returned, so that he was now alone in the world. Soon after this Peter and Clement make an excursion to the island of Aradus, where a beggar woman, telling the story of her life, proves to be Clement's mother. Resuming their journey, they come to Laodicea, the mother accompanying them. Here the repetition of her story leads to the recognition of Niceta and Aquila as the twin brothers of Clement, who, after they had been shipwrecked with their mother, had been picked up and sold as slaves. After this Peter and the three brothers meet on the sea-shore an old man poorly clad, who yet proves to be very learned, and who enters into a discussion with the Christians which continues several days. His favorite doctrine is that of *genesis*, a doctrine of fates, in illustration of which he tells the story of his own life; how, owing to a certain conjunction of the stars, his wife had been compelled to commit adultery with a slave, and to sail away to meet her death by shipwreck. This leads to explanations and another recognition, the old man proving to be Faustinianus, the husband and father of the long separated family. After this we have a discourse by Clement on the heathen mythology, and then an account of the transformation of Faustinianus by the magic of Simon Magus, so that his face is the counterpart of Simon's. Peter, after using this false appearance to work harm to Simon, restores to Faustinianus his own face; the latter is baptized, and all ends happily. [In the "Homilies" the main disputation between Peter and Simon occurs here at Laodicea, Clement's father acting as umpire.]

This narrative as it appears in the "Homilies" is preceded by two letters: one from Peter to James, saying that the teachings of the book are to be withheld from the multitude; and one from Clement to James, announcing Peter's martyrdom and his own succession to the bishopric of Rome.

DOCTRINE OF THE WORKS.

Both are Ebionitic, but the "Homilies" are the more pronounced. Judaism and Christianity, according to the "Homilies," are substantially the same; to receive either Moses or Christ is sufficient. In the "Recognitions" both must be received. The "Homilies" reject sacrifices utterly, declaring the passages of Scripture favoring them to be corrupt. The "Recognitions" say that sacrifices were divinely prescribed until the true Prophet should replace them by baptism. The "Homilies" say that the true Prophet had been incarnate repeatedly, first in Adam and lastly in Jesus. The "Recognitions" only teach that he had revealed himself to and inspired other holy men. The dignity of Christ is greater here than in the "Homilies"; but neither work gives Him the New Testament rank.

These works have been deemed of great importance by writers of the Tübingen school, as contributing to their theory that the primitive Christianity was extremely Judaistic (Petrine), and that, after a sharp contest, it was supplanted by the present (Pauline) faith.

THE APOSTOLICAL CONSTITUTIONS.

The "Apostolical Constitutions" is a collection of ecclesiastical regulations purporting to come from the Apostles. It is composed of eight books, not all of like origin. Their value has been very variously estimated. Whiston claimed that they were "the most sacred of the canonical books of the New Testament," having been "delivered at Jerusalem, and in Mt. Sion, by our Saviour to the eleven apostles there assembled after the resurrection"; while most writers bring their date down into the neighborhood of the Nicene age, and some place it as late as the fifth and sixth centuries. There are three parts to the work: 1, the first six books; 2, the seventh book; and 3, the eighth book. Book seventh is thought to be a rewriting of books first to sixth, perhaps as a summary or appendix. Book eighth has been identified by Bunsen with the work of Hippolytus on "Gifts." At the close of this book are found

THE APOSTOLICAL CANONS.

These are a collection of fifty (Western Church) or eighty-five (Eastern Church) ecclesiastical canons, purporting to come from the Holy Apostles. The Eastern Church regards them as genuine and authoritative; the Roman Church does not. Their compilation in the present form dates from A. D. 500 in the West, and from A. D. 550 in the East. As to the origin of their contents, opinions differ. Bishop Beveridge, a conservative writer, while not claiming their apostolic origin, contended that they were the decrees of synods of the latter part of the second or early part of the third century, and that they were formed into a codex in the third century. Von Drey thinks the fifty canons were collected in the early part of the fifth century, partly from decrees of Post-Nicene councils, partly from the "Constitutions," the other thirty-five canons having been added later.

IGNATIUS OF ANTIOCH.

THE evident antiquity of certain of the so-called Ignatian letters, and the important place which these letters have held in ecclesiastical discussions, have given to Ignatius himself a prominence which he would not otherwise hold. This father, as we learn from Eusebius, was the second bishop of Antioch after Peter. We know nothing certain of his history, save that of his last days, though the "Acts of Martyrdom" declare that he was a disciple of the Apostle John. "Tradition says [Euseb., "Eccl. Hist.," iii. 36] that he was sent away from Syria to Rome, and was cast as food to wild beasts, on account of his testimony to Christ; and that being carried through Asia under a most rigid custody, he fortified the different churches in the cities where he tarried by his discourses and exhortations, particularly cautioning them against the heresies which even then were springing up and prevailing. He exhorted them to adhere firmly to the tradition of the apostles; which, for the sake of greater security, he deemed it necessary to attest by committing it to writing." Eusebius mentions by name seven epistles — to the Ephesians, the Magnesians, the Trallians, the Romans, the Philadelphians, the Smyrneans, and to Polycarp—which he says were written by Ignatius, on his way to Rome. For the particulars of his martyrdom, we have only the questionable testimony of the "Acts of Martyrdom of Ignatius," of which we have no trace before the sixth century, though Irenæus refers to the fact of his having been condemned to the wild beasts. The date most commonly assigned to the martyrdom is Dec. 20, A. D. 116. The legends as to Ignatius's having been taken into Christ's arms when a child, and as to his having had a vision of angels singing antiphonally to the Holy Trinity, are only legends.

The Ignatian epistles have long been divided into two classes, known as the genuine and the spurious epistles. The former class has commonly embraced the seven letters mentioned by Eusebius, and these are known to us, in Greek, in two forms, the longer and the shorter recensions. Of these, the first was the earlier known to modern scholars; but the manifest corruption of the text led to researches by Archbishop Usher, which resulted in the discovery, first of two Latin texts, and then of a Greek text, of the shorter recension. These were published, the Latin in 1644 by Usher, and the Greek in 1646 by Vossius; and in time they had come to be regarded by most scholars as the genuine letters of Ignatius, the longer form being looked upon as an interpolation. After two hundred years, however, a new discovery was made, which again left the "Ignatian question" an open one. This was the finding at a Nitrian convent in 1843 of two very ancient Syriac manuscripts of the Ignatian epistles. Instead of the seven epistles of the Vossian collection, these manuscripts contained only three, the epistles to Polycarp, to the Ephesians, and to the Romans, and these in a shorter form than that of the Greek collection. These three were confidently claimed by their first editor, Cureton, and by Bunsen, who also edited them, to be *the* epistles of Ignatius, as opposed to the seven Vossian epistles. Into the discussion which this claim awakened, or into the more recent discussions which have followed upon the discovery of an Armenian translation from the Syriac of all seven of the epistles, it is not needful here to enter. It is sufficient to say that, in preparing this book, the judgment of Bishop Lightfoot, as expressed in his review of "Supernatural Religion," has been deemed a safe one. This judgment was that the three Curetonian epistles might be confidently received as *genuine*, and that the seven Vossian epistles might be looked upon as authoritative for the middle of the second century. Guided by this principle, our text presents, as the indisputably genuine works of Ignatius, the three short or Syriac epistles. Bunsen's translation has been preferred to the Curetonian, and is given without change.

THE THREE EPISTLES OF ST. IGNATIUS.

A.—*The Epistle to Polycarp.*

Ignatius [who also is Theophoros] to Polycarp, overseer of the Smyrneans, who rather is overseen by God the Father and the Lord Jesus Christ, much greeting.

1. Heartily welcoming thy mind, which in God is founded as upon an immovable rock, I praise God the more abundantly for having been accounted worthy to behold thy unblamable countenance, of which may I have to rejoice in God! I beseech thee, by the grace with which thou art clothed, that thou add to thy course, and exhort all men to be saved. Make thy office to be respected with all diligence both of body and spirit. Be careful for unanimity, than which there is nothing more excellent. Bear all men even as the Lord beareth thee. Have patience with all in love, even as thou doest. Be instant in prayer. Ask for more understanding than thou hast. Watch, for thou hast already a spirit that sleepeth not. Speak to every one accord-

ing to the manner in which God speaketh. Bear the infirmities of all men like a perfect athlete; for where there is much labor, much also is the gain. If thou love the good disciples only, thou hast no grace; rather subdue by meekness those who are evil. All wounds are not healed by one salve. Allay paroxysm by embrocation. Be wise as the serpent in everything, and harmless as the dove. For this reason art thou both of flesh and of spirit, that thou mayest be persuasive as to those things which appear to thee before thy face, and mayest ask for the things invisible that they may be revealed to thee, in order that thou mayest be deficient in nothing and mayest abound in all gifts; which it is time thou shouldest pray for, as the pilot for the wind, and as he who is tossed by the tempest for the harbor, that thou mayest attain God. Be vigilant as God's athlete. The meed is incorruptibility and life eternal, of which things thou also art persuaded. In everything I pledge for thy soul myself and my bonds, which thou hast loved. Let not those confound thee who, appearing worthy of truth, teach strange doctrines. Stand in the truth like an anvil which is struck, for it becomes a great athlete to be struck and to conquer. More especially on God's account it behooveth us to endure everything, that he also may endure us. Be careful more than thou art. Be discerning of the times. Expect him who is above times, him to whom there are no times, him who is unseen, him who for our sakes became seen, him who is impalpable, him who is without suffering, him who for our sakes suffered, him who for our sakes endured everything in every form.

2. Let not the widows be neglected; after our Lord be thou their guardian. Let nothing be done without thy will, neither do thou anything without the will of God; nor indeed doest thou. Stand

well. Let the meetings be more frequent; seek to know every man personally. Despise not the slaves, male and female, neither let them be puffed up; but as for the glory of God let them work more, that they may be meet for that more excellent liberty which is of God. Let them not desire to be redeemed from the common stock, that they may not be found the slaves of lust. Fly the coquetting women, but the more hold converse with the aged matrons. Say to my sisters that they love the Lord, and that they be content with their husbands in body and spirit. Likewise charge my brothers in the name of our Lord Jesus Christ, that they love their wives as the Lord his church. If a man be able to continue in chastity of body for the honor of our Lord, let him continue without boasting; if he boast, he is lost: if he have made it known to anybody except the bishop, he is gone into perdition. It is becoming to men and women who marry, that they be married by the counsel of the bishop, that the marriage may be made according to the Lord and not according to lust. Let everything be done for the honor of God.

3. Keep ye to the bishop, that God also may keep to you. I pledge my soul for those who are subject to the bishop and the presbyters and deacons: may my portion with God be with them! Labor together, struggle together, run together, go to sleep together, rise together as God's stewards and intimate friends and ministers. Please him under whom you serve, from whom you also receive the wages. Let no man be found a deserter. Let your baptism be to you as armor, and faith as a helmet, and love as a spear, and patience as a panoply. Let your credit be your good works, that ye may get paid out what is worthy of you. Have patience in meekness as God has with you. May I have to rejoice in you at all times! The Christian has not

power over himself, but is in the service of God. I salute him who is deemed worthy to go to Antioch in my stead, as I charged thee.

B.—*The Epistle to the Ephesians.*

Ignatius [who also is Theophoros] to the church which is blessed in the greatness and fullness of the Father, to her *who is* preordained before the world to be for ever unto lasting and unchangeable glory, perfected and elected in a true purpose in the will of the Father of Jesus Christ our God; to the most blissworthy church which is in Ephesus, all hail in Jesus Christ in pure joy!

1. Since I have received in God that much-loved manifestation which you have rightmindedly made according to the faith and love in Jesus Christ our Saviour, because, as those who imitate God, you have been excited in your blood fully to accomplish the Godlike work; for when you had heard that I was bound *and prevented* from visiting *you* on account of our common name and hope, trusting in your prayer (to obtain) to be thrown among the beasts at Rome, in order that by achieving this I might be enabled to be a disciple of God, you have made haste to see me—since, therefore, I have in the name of God received the visit of all of you in the person of one, nay, *who* in unspeakable love *is* your bishop—and I pray in Jesus Christ that you may love him and that you may all be like him, for blessed is he who has vouchsafed you to be worthy of having such a bishop—since, then, love does not allow me to be silent toward you, on this account I have chosen to exhort you to conform to the will of God. For when no lust worketh in you with power to torment you, ye live according to God. Your off-scouring is also your sanctification, O Ephesians! Ye of that church which is renowned in the

world! Carnal men can not do spiritual things, nor spiritual men carnal things; just as faith can not do the things of unbelief, nor unbelief those of faith. But even the works you do according to the flesh are spiritual works; for you do all in Jesus Christ, prepared *as you are* for the building of God the Father, carried up to the height through the engine of Jesus Christ which is the cross, using the Holy Spirit as the rope, while faith is the pulley and love the way carrying up to God.

2. As to other men, pray for them—for there is hope of their repenting—that they may be partakers of God. Give them opportunity of becoming your disciples even by your works. Against their lofty words put humility, and against their blaspheming meekness in constant prayers, against their seduction firmness in the faith, against their violence mildness; not striving to imitate them. But by meekness let us strive to be imitators of the Lord, than whom who was ever more wronged? or deprived? or depressed? For it is not a question of promise, but whether one be found in the strength of faith even unto the end. Rather than to speak and to be nothing, it is better to be silent and to be *something*, in order that one may work by what one speaks, and may be known by what one is silent about.

3. My spirit boweth down before the cross, which is a scandal to the unbelieving, but to us salvation and life eternal. Thus were hidden from the prince of this world the virginity of Mary, and the birth and death of the Lord; three shouting mysteries *were* operated in God's quietness. From *the appearance of* the star and the manifestation thereby of the Son, every magic power disappeared, and every bond was dissolved, and the old kingdom, and the ignorance of wickedness perished. From that time everything was put in commotion,

because the dissolution of death was meditated, and what was ordained with God took its beginning.

C.—*The Epistle to the Romans.*

Ignatius [who also is Theophoros] to the church which has found mercy by the greatness of the Father most high, to her who presides in dignity over the country of the Romans, to her who is worthy of God and is worthy of her honorable position, worthy of being called blessed, worthy of praise and worthy that her prayer be heard, who excelleth before all in love, and hath Christ for her law blamelessly, much greeting!

1. Having long since prayed to God that I might be worthy to see your God-worthy faces, I now hope that I shall salute you, *being* bound in Jesus Christ, if it be God's will that I should be deemed worthy of God to the end. For the beginning has been well disposed, if I attain to receive without hindrance my portion at last by suffering. For I am fearful of your love, lest it should injure me. For to you it is easy to do whatsoever you please; but for me, it is difficult that I should attain God, if indeed you do not spare me. For I shall not have such opportunity to attain God; nor will ye, if ye now be silent, ever have the benefit of a better work. If ye keep silence about me, I shall become God's speech; but if ye love my body, I shall be again an echo of myself. Do not try to give me anything better than this, that I should be sacrificed to God whilst the altar is prepared, that ye, becoming a loving choir, may praise the Father in Christ Jesus that he deemed the bishop worthy to be God's, when he called him from the rising *of the sun* to the setting. It is good that I should set from the world to God, that I may rise into him. Ye have never envied any man. Ye have taught

others. Only pray for strength from within and from without, that I may not only speak, but also may will; that I may not be called only a Christian, but also may be found to be one: for if I am found to be, I am also fit to be called, faithful even when not appearing in the world. Nothing, indeed, that *is only* appearing is good: for Christianity is not a work of persuasion, but of high-mindedness, when hated by the world.

2. I write to the churches, and I declare to all, that willingly I die for God, if it be that you hinder me not. I beg of you, do not become to me an unseasonable love. Let me be of the beasts, by whose means I am enabled to obtain God. I am God's wheat, and by the teeth of the beasts am I ground, that I may be found God's pure bread. Rather entreat kindly the beasts that they may be a grave for me, and may leave nothing of my body; that not even when I am fallen asleep, I may be a burden upon any man. Then I shall be in truth a disciple of Jesus Christ, when the world seeth not even my body. Supplicate our Lord for me, that by these instruments I may be found a sacrifice to God. I am not commanding you like Peter and Paul: they were apostles, I am a condemned convict; they were free, I am hitherto a slave. But if I suffer, I am a freed man of Jesus Christ, and I shall rise from the dead, in him, a free man.

3. And now, since I am in bonds, I learn to desire nothing. From Syria to Rome I am cast among beasts, by sea and by land, by night and by day; since I am bound between ten leopards, who get worse when I do good to them. But by their ill treatment I am furthered in my apprenticeship: still by that I am not justified. May I have to rejoice of the beasts prepared for me! and I pray that they may be found ready for me, and I will kindly entreat them quickly to devour me, and not,

as they have done to some, being afraid of them, to keep from touching me. And should they not be willing, I will force them.

4. Pardon me: what is expedient for me, I know myself. Let nothing envy me, neither things visible nor invisible, that I may attain Jesus Christ. Fire and the cross, scattering of the bones and the array of the beasts, the mutilation of the limbs and the grinding of the whole body—hard torments of the devil!—let them come upon me, if only I may attain Jesus Christ. The pains of child-birth await me: my love is crucified, and there is no fire in me to love matter. I do not desire the food of corruption, nor the desires of this world. The bread of God I seek, which is the body of Christ; and as drink I seek his blood, which is love incorruptible.

5. My spirit saluteth you, and the love of the churches which have received me as for the name of Jesus Christ. For also those who are not bodily near to the road accompanied me in every city. And now that I am near to Rome, I meditate many things in God; but I moderate myself, that I may not perish through boasting; for now it is becoming in me that I should fear the more abundantly, and should not look to those that puff me up. For those who say to me "Martyr," scourge me: it is true that I desire to suffer, but I do not know if I be worthy. For my zeal is not apparent to many, but it wars within me. I want, therefore, meekness; because by that the prince of this world is made powerless. I am able to write to you heavenly things; but I fear lest I should do you harm (pardon me), that, not being able to take it in, you might be choked. For even I, for being in bonds and able to know heavenly things, and the places of angels and the station of powers and the things visible and invisible, am for all that not a dis-

ciple: for I lack much of being perfected for God. Farewell to the end, in the patience of Jesus Christ.

POLYCARP OF SMYRNA.

IF Clement attracts us by a certain vague grandeur of his person, if Ignatius invites our attention by the sharp outlines of his ecclesiastical teachings, Polycarp of Smyrna compels our regard by the unique importance of his position. For his life spans with one grand arch the entire chasm of historic uncertainty which appears in our accounts of the early church. One firm abutment rests upon the Apostle John, the other, as secure, rests upon the well-known Irenæus; and over this solid structure is borne down in security the stream of apostolic traditions. In vain did the turbid waters of the second-century heresies seek to pollute the stream; in vain do modern scholars contend that the stream which reached Irenæus was one of mingled waters, flowing from diverse fountains. Irenæus himself says, Nay, it was one stream, flowing from one source over this single life.

Irenæus, having been the pupil of Polycarp, gives testimony of him which is entirely trustworthy. In a letter to an early companion he says: "For I remember the occurrences of those days better than the more recent; so that I can tell even the spot in which the blessed Polycarp sat and conversed, and his outgoings and incomings, and the character of his life, and the form of his body, and the conversations which he held with the multitude; and how he related his familiar intercourse with John and the rest who had seen the Lord, and how he rehearsed their sayings, and what things they were which he had heard from them with regard to the Lord and his miracles and teaching. All these things Polycarp related in harmony with the writings, as having received them from the eyewitnesses of the Word of life. These things then I was in the habit of eagerly hearing through the mercy given me by God, storing them up, not on paper, but in my heart." Again he says: "And Polycarp, who was not only instructed by apostles, and had intercourse with many who had seen Christ, but was also appointed for Asia by apostles, in the church that is in Smyrna, an overseer, whom also we have seen in the beginning of our life, for he remained a long time and at an exceeding old age, having borne his testimony gloriously and most notably, departed this life, always taught these things, which also he gave to the church, and which alone are true." He further gives account of Polycarp's earnest opposition to the heretic Marcion; also of his visit to Rome in the time of Anicetus, and the friendly variance of Polycarp and Anicetus with respect to the observance of Easter.

In regard to the writings of his early teacher Irenæus speaks explicitly. Alluding to certain doctrines, he says: "This also can be proved from his letters which he (Polycarp) sent either to the neighboring churches, confirming them, or to some of the brethren, warning them and urging them on." Again: "There is also a letter of Polycarp's written to the Philippians, of a most satisfactory nature, from which also those who are willing and have a care about their salvation can learn the character of his faith, and the proclamation of the truth."

How few characters of antiquity, whether secular or ecclesiastical, have such testimony from an actual pupil to their person and works! Surely, when we talk of Polycarp, we may feel ourselves to be upon historic ground. This apart from the testimony given in the "Martyrium of Polycarp," a document purporting to be a letter from the church at Smyrna to a neighboring church, giving an account of the martyrdom of their bishop. This is the most ancient of all the *Martyria*, and has commonly been regarded as a genuine work of the Smyrnean Church. It was so regarded by Eusebius, who embodied most of it in his history. The account is a detailed one of how, in a time of persecution, Polycarp was persuaded to leave the city, but, being betrayed by a servant, was brought back and put to death in the stadium, after having nobly confessed Christ. Various incidents of this story have been subjected to such adverse criticism that we may not safely press its accuracy in details; yet both external and internal evidence lead to the opinion that in outline (even if largely interpolated) it is true. Certain chronological notes appended to this "Martyrium" by a later writer, though still a very early one, declare the martyrdom to have occurred in the spring-time of the proconsulship of Statius Quadratus. This is shown by the most recent investigations to have been in the year 155. This date, allowing him to have died at the age of eighty-six years, as given in the "Martyrium," would fix his birth in A. D. 69. Assigning the death of John to the very earliest conjectured date, Polycarp must still have been of an age sufficient to comprehend and hand down in their purity the teachings of John and the other apostles. These teachings, he told Irenæus, were "in harmony with the writings"; by which Irenæus, who had substantially our canon, meant the Scriptures which we read to-day.

The Epistle of Polycarp to the Philippians is, as we have seen, most satisfactorily attested, though certain chapters are known only in a Latin version. Its integrity has been questioned, the genuineness of chapter thirteen being denied; but such scholars as Zahn (whose text has here been followed) and Lightfoot claim that the whole epistle is the work of Polycarp. Granting its integrity, its date can not be much later than A. D. 116, the time of Ignatius's death. No other remains of Polycarp's writings have come down to us.

THE EPISTLE OF POLYCARP TO THE PHILIPPIANS.

Polycarp and the presbyters that are with him to the church of God which is at Philippi: Mercy unto you, and peace from God Almighty, and the Lord Jesus Christ our Saviour, be multiplied.

1. I rejoiced greatly with you, in our Lord Jesus Christ, that ye received the patterns of true love, and accompanied, as it behooved you, those who were bound with chains, the fitting ornament of saints, the crowns of those who are truly chosen of God and our Lord; and that the firm root of your faith, which was preached from ancient times, re-

mains until now, and brings forth fruit to our Lord Jesus Christ, who suffered himself to be brought even to death for our sins: *whom God raised up, having loosed the pains of death: in whom, not seeing, ye believe, with joy unspeakable and full of glory.* Into which joy many desire to enter, knowing that *by grace ye are saved, not of works*, but by the will of God, through Jesus Christ.

2. *Wherefore, girding up your loins*, serve God in fear and truth, laying aside all empty and vain speech, and the error of many, *believing in him that raised up our Lord Jesus Christ from the dead, and gave him glory*, and a throne at his right hand; to whom all things in heaven and earth are subject; whom every living creature worships; who comes to be the judge of the quick and the dead; whose blood God shall require of them that believe not in him. But he that raised him up from the dead shall raise up us also, if we do his will, and walk in his commandments, and love the things which he loved; abstaining from all unrighteousness, inordinate affection, love of money, evil speaking, false witness; *not rendering evil for evil, or railing for railing*, or blow for blow, or curse for curse; but remembering what the Lord taught us, saying, *Judge not, that ye be not judged; forgive, and it shall be forgiven unto you; be merciful, that ye may obtain mercy: for with the measure that ye mete withal, it shall be measured to you again;* and that *Blessed are the poor, and they that are persecuted for righteousness' sake; for theirs is the kingdom of God.*

3. I have not assumed to myself, brethren, the liberty of writing to you those things concerning righteousness; but ye yourselves before encouraged me. For neither can I, nor any other such as I am, come up to the wisdom of the blessed and renowned Paul, who, being among you, in the presence of those who then lived, taught with exactness and

soundness the word of truth; who in his absence also wrote an epistle to you, into which if ye diligently look, ye may be able to be edified in the faith delivered unto you, *which is the mother of us all*, being followed with hope and led on by love, both toward God and Christ, and toward our neighbor. For if any one hath these things within himself, he hath fulfilled the law of righteousness; for he that hath charity is far from all sin.

4. But *the love of money is the beginning of all evils.* Knowing, therefore, that *we brought nothing into the world, neither are we able to carry anything out,* let us arm ourselves with the armor of righteousness, and teach ourselves first to walk in the commandment of the Lord: then also [teach] your wives [to walk] in the faith and love and purity which is given unto them, loving their own husbands in all truth, and kindly affectionate to all others equally in all temperance, and to bring up their children in the instruction and fear of God: [teach] that the widows be sober as to what concerns the faith of the Lord, praying without ceasing for all men, being far from all detraction, evil-speaking, false witness, love of money, and all evil; knowing that they are the altar of God, and that he sees all blemishes, and nothing is hid from him, either of words or thoughts, nor any of the secret things of the heart.

5. Knowing, therefore, that *God is not mocked*, we ought to walk worthy both of his command and of his glory. In like manner the deacons must be blameless in the sight of his righteousness, as the ministers of God and Christ, and not of men: not false accusers, not double-tongued, not lovers of money, temperate in all things, compassionate, careful, walking according to the truth of the Lord, who became the servant of all; whom if we please in this present world, we shall be made partakers

also of that which is to come, according as he hath promised to us that he will raise us from the dead: and that if we shall walk worthy of him, we shall also reign together with him, if we believe. In like manner the young men must be blameless in all things, above all taking care of their purity, and restraining themselves from all evil. For it is good to emerge out of the lusts which are in the world: for every *lust warreth against the spirit;* and *neither fornicators, nor effeminate, nor abusers of themselves with mankind shall inherit the kingdom of God*, neither they which act foolishly. Wherefore, it is necessary that ye abstain from all these things, being subject to the presbyters and deacons, as unto God and Christ. The virgins also should walk in a spotless and pure conscience.

6. Let the elders also be compassionate, merciful to all, bringing back such as are in error, seeking out all those that are weak, not neglecting the widow or the fatherless, or the poor; but *providing always what is good in the sight of God and men:* abstaining from all wrath, respect of persons, and unrighteous judgment; being far from all covetousness; not ready to believe anything against any; not severe in judgment, knowing that we are all debtors in point of sin. If therefore we pray to the Lord that he would forgive us, we ought also to forgive. For we are before the eyes of our Lord and God, and *must all stand before the judgment seat of Christ, and must every one give an account of himself.* Let us therefore so serve him, with fear and all reverence, as he himself hath commanded, and as the apostles who have preached the gospel unto us, and the prophets who have foretold the coming of our Lord [have taught us]: being zealous of what is good, abstaining from all offense, and from false brethren, and from those who bear the name of Christ in hypocrisy, who deceive vain men.

7. *For whosoever confesses not that Jesus Christ is come in the flesh is antichrist;* and whosoever confesses not the suffering of the cross is of the devil; and whosoever perverts the oracles of the Lord to his own lusts, and says there is neither resurrection nor judgment, he is the first-born of Satan. Wherefore, leaving the vanity of many, and the false doctrines, let us return to the word which was delivered to us from the beginning, *watching unto prayer*, and persevering in fasting; with supplication beseeching the all-seeing God *not to lead us into temptation*, as the Lord hath said, *The spirit indeed is willing, but the flesh is weak.*

8. Let us therefore without ceasing hold steadfastly to him who is our hope, and the earnest of our righteousness, even Jesus Christ, *who bore our sins in his own body on the tree; who did no sin, neither was guile found in his mouth;* but endured all for our sakes, that we might live through him. Let us therefore imitate his patience; and if we suffer for his name, let us glorify him. For this example he hath given us by himself, and so we have believed.

9. I exhort you all therefore to obey the word of righteousness, and exercise all patience, which ye have seen set forth before your eyes, not only in the blessed Ignatius, and Zosimus, and Rufus, but also in others among yourselves, and in Paul himself, and the other apostles; being confident of this, that all these have *not run in vain*, but in faith and righteousness; and that they are gone to the place which was due to them, in the presence of the Lord, with whom also they suffered. For they loved not this present world, but him that died for us, and was raised again by God for our sake.

[* 10. Stand therefore in these things, and follow the example of the Lord, being firm and immutable

* From the Latin version.

in the faith, lovers of the brotherhood, lovers of one another, companions together in the truth, exhibiting toward each other the *sweet reasonableness* of the Lord, despising none. When it is in your power to do good, defer it not; *for charity delivereth from death.* Be all of you subject one to another, *having your conversation honest among the gentiles, that by your good works* both ye yourselves may receive praise, and the Lord may not be blasphemed through you. *But woe to him by whom the name of the Lord is blasphemed.* Wherefore teach all men sobriety, in which do ye also exercise yourselves.

11. I am greatly afflicted for Valens, who was once made a presbyter among you; that he should so little understand the place that was given unto him. Wherefore I admonish you that ye abstain from cupidity, and that ye be chaste and true of speech. Keep yourselves from all evil. For he that in these things can not govern himself, how shall he be able to prescribe them to another? If a man doth not keep himself from concupiscence, he shall be polluted with idolatry, and he shall be judged as if of the gentiles, who are ignorant of the judgment of the Lord. *Do we not know that the saints shall judge the world?* as Paul teaches. But I have neither perceived nor heard anything of the kind in you, among whom the blessed Paul labored, and who are [named] in the beginning of his epistle. For he glories of you in all the churches which alone had then known God; for we [in Smyrna] had not yet known him. Wherefore, brethren, I am exceedingly sorry both for him (Valens) and for his wife: to whom may the Lord grant true repentance. And be ye then moderate on this occasion; and *consider not such as enemies,* but call them back, as suffering and erring members, that ye may save your whole body. For by so doing ye edify yourselves.

12. For I trust that ye are well exercised in the Holy Scriptures, and that nothing is hid from you: but to me it is not granted [to edify you]. Only, as it is written in the Scriptures, *Be ye angry and sin not*, and *Let not the sun go down upon your wrath*. Blessed is he that remembereth, which I trust to be true of you. Now the God and Father of our Lord Jesus Christ, and he himself who is our everlasting High Priest, the Son of God, even Jesus Christ, build you up in faith and truth, and in all meekness and lenity, and in patience and long-suffering, and forbearance and chastity: and grant unto you a lot and portion among his saints, and unto us with you, and unto all that are under heaven, who shall believe in our Lord Jesus Christ, and in his Father who raised him from the dead. Pray for all the saints. Pray also for kings, and authorities, and princes, and for those who persecute you and hate you, and for the enemies of the cross; that your fruit may be manifest in all, and that ye may be perfect in Him.]

13. Both ye and Ignatius wrote to me, that if any one went [hence] into Syria, he should carry with him what was written by you; which I will attend to, if I have a convenient opportunity, either by myself, or by him whom I shall send acting for me and upon your account. The epistles of Ignatius which he wrote unto us, and others as many as we have with us, we have sent to you, according to your order; which are subjoined to this epistle: from which ye may be greatly profited. For they treat of faith and patience, and of all things which pertain to edification in our Lord.

[* What ye know more certainly of Ignatius, and those that are with him, signify unto us.

14. These things have I written unto you by Crescens, whom up to this day I have recommended to you, and do now recommend. For he hath had

* From the Latin version.

his conversation without blame among us, and I trust in like manner also with you. You will also have regard unto his sister when she shall come unto you. Be ye safe in the Lord Jesus Christ: and his grace be with you all. Amen.]

BARNABAS.

THAT there existed very early in the history of the church a letter written by one Barnabas, and that that letter has come down to us, there can be little doubt. Who Barnabas was, however, we do not know. The early writers, beginning with Clement of Alexandria, identify him with Barnabas the companion of Paul; but that supposition is disproved by the epistle itself. Barnabas the Cyprian was a Levite, and was of course familiar with the Jewish rites—probably practiced some of them to the end of his life; he must also, from his presence at the apostolic council at Jerusalem, in which that subject was discussed, have known perfectly the opinions of the twelve as to the relation of Judaism to Christianity. But the epistle was written by one who not simply distorts, but makes gross errors concerning, common Jewish observances; and by one who, instead of regarding Judaism as the legitimate predecessor of Christianity—the Law a schoolmaster to lead to Christ—as did the apostles, represents the Jews as entirely wrong in ever having observed the ceremonial law. This of itself would disprove the early tradition; but it may be added that the epistle declares all Syrians to have been circumcised, a mistake which could not have been made by one who had resided long at Antioch; that it was written subsequent to A. D. 70, whereas Barnabas the Cyprian is thought to have died before A. D. 62; and that it betrays a style of reckless allegorizing utterly foreign to one who had consorted with the apostles, not to say with our Lord himself. There is little satisfaction in thus showing who was not the author, but this is almost the only certain thing we can say. It is supposed by most critics, however, that it was written by a Gentile Christian who was either a resident of Alexandria or lived within Alexandrian influence. Evidence of this is seen in the allegorizing tone of the epistle, and in the importance it attaches to *knowledge* (γνῶσις) as contrasted with *faith* (πίστις), which features were characteristics of that school of thought. The readers for whom it was intended are conjectured to have been Alexandrian Christians, who were in danger of being drawn away into Jewish practices; though Origen calls it a catholic epistle, that is intended for general circulation. Its date is uncertain. It can not have been earlier than the destruction of Jerusalem. It would seem also to have been quoted by Celsus —the passage calling the apostles *sinners above all sin*—about the middle of the second century. Between these dates we have but slight indications of a definite time, though what we have point to the first quarter of the century, from A. D. 119 to 126.

The epistle is in two parts, chaps. 1-17 and 18-21, which are somewhat dissimilar in style; but both parts are quoted by Clement, and there is no sufficient reason to question its integrity. The whole epistle is found in Greek, in one of the most ancient extant manuscripts, the *Codex Sinaiticus*, (*cir.* A. D. 350), in which it follows the canonical books. The semi-canonical character thus indicated was accorded to the letter by both Clement and Origen. The latest critical text is that of Gebhardt, by which the translation here used has been amended. The italicized words are supplied. Quotations have their appropriate marks. Attention is called to but a single passage at the close of chapter iv.: "As it is written, 'many called but few chosen.'"

THE EPISTLE OF BARNABAS.

1. Joy be with you, sons and daughters, in the name of the Lord who loved us in peace. Seeing that God's just requirements are great and abounding to you ward, I rejoice exceedingly and beyond measure in your blessed and glorious spirits; in such manner have ye received the engrafted grace of the free gift of the Spirit. Wherefore also I the more rejoice in mine own *heart*, hoping to be saved, because that I truly perceive within you the spirit of the Lord's love poured forth from his riches upon you. With so great *joy* concerning you hath the desired sight of you moved me. Being persuaded therefore of this, and convinced in my own *mind*—for having spoken many things among you, I know that the Lord hath been my companion in the way of righteousness, and am utterly constrained also myself to this, namely, to love you above my own soul, for great faith and love dwell within you in hope of his life—accounting this therefore, that if I am at pains concerning you to impart some

portion of that whereof I have received, that to minister to such spirits will be to me *not without* reward, I made haste shortly to send unto you, that ye might have your knowledge (γνῶσις) perfected with your faith (πίστις). There are then three revelations of the Lord: our hope of life, its beginning, its end; and the beginning of faith is righteousness, and the end *thereof* love, the work of gladness and exultation in witness of righteousness. For the master hath revealed to us by the prophets that which is past and that which is at hand, and hath given us also the first fruits of the taste of that which shall be. Of which things we behold the gradual accomplishment, according as he hath said, and ought with the more abundance and uplifting of heart to draw near to his altar. I then, not as a teacher but as one of your own selves, will show forth a few things, by the which in the present *time of trial* ye shall be made glad.

2. [The Jewish sacrifices are now abolished under the new law of Jesus Christ.]

3. [Showing that the fasts observed by the Jews are not true fasts acceptable to God.]

4. [The final offense concerning which it is written is at hand. We must not err by] saying that the covenant belongs to them (the Jews) and us *also*. To us *it belongeth;* but they lost it thus utterly, though Moses once received it. [We must avoid iniquity, lest we be judged as Israel has been.] Let us take heed lest so be that we be found, as it is written, "many called but few chosen."

5. For to this end the Lord endured to deliver up his flesh to destruction, that we might be cleansed by the remission of sins, which is in the blood of his sprinkling .... Is. liii. 5–7 .... [Christ] that he might abolish death and show forth the resurrection from the dead, since it behooved him to be manifested in the flesh, endured *suffering* that

he might restore the promise to the fathers, and might himself prepare his new people for himself, and by being upon the earth show forth that when he hath himself accomplished the resurrection he will judge *mankind* . . . . And when he chose out his own apostles who should preach his gospel, who, that he might show that "He came not to call the righteous but sinners," were transgressors above all sin, then did he manifest himself to be the Son of God . . . . [He came also to bring to a head the sins of the Jews.]

6. [Various prophecies, e. g., that of the stone rejected by the builders, explained by gnosis.]

7. [Fasting, and the goat sent away, shown to be types of Christ. The chapter closes with these words:] Thus, he (Jesus) saith, they who would see me, and lay hold of my kingdom, must through tribulation and suffering obtain me.

8. But what type think ye it is, that it hath been commanded to Israel, that those men in whom sins are at the full should offer a heifer, and slay and burn it, and that children should take up the ash, and cast it into vessels, and bind the scarlet wool upon wood (behold again the type of the cross and the scarlet wool) and hyssop *therewith*, and that after this manner the children should sprinkle the people one by one, that they may be purified from their sins? Consider how in *all* simplicity it is said unto you, The calf is Jesus; the men who make offering, *being* sinners, *are they* who offered him for the slaughter. [But now the men are no longer *guilty*, are no longer regarded as sinners.]* But the boys who sprinkle are they who preached unto us the gospel of the remission of sins and the purification of the heart, unto whom, being twelve *in number* for a witness of the tribes—for there are twelve tribes in Israel—he gave authority over the

* Doubtful text.

gospel, that they should preach it. But wherefore are the boys that sprinkle three *in number?* For a testimony unto Abraham, Isaac, and Jacob, because these are mighty before God. And why the wool upon the wood? Because the kingdom of Jesus is *established* upon wood, and they that hope upon him shall live for ever. But wherefore the wool withal and the hyssop? Because in his kingdom there shall be days evil and polluted, in the which we shall be saved. For he that is sick in the flesh is healed by the pollution of the hyssop. And therefore are the things which were so done clear unto us, but unto them dark, because they have not heard the voice of the Lord.

9. Furthermore, he saith concerning the ears, how that our circumcision is of the heart. The Lord saith in the prophet, "To the hearing of the ear they did obey me." And again he saith, "With hearing shall they that are afar off hear, they shall know what things I have done." And "Be ye circumcised," saith the Lord, "in your hearts." And again he saith, "Hear, O Israel, that the Lord thy God saith these things." And again the Spirit of the Lord prophesieth, "Who is he that will live for ever? With hearing let him hear the voice of my Son." And again he saith, "Hear, O heaven, and give ear, O earth, for the Lord hath spoken these things for a testimony." And again he saith, "Hear the word of the Lord, ye rulers of this people." And again he saith, "Hear, ye children, the voice of one crying in the wilderness." So then he circumcised our hearings, that we might hear the word and believe. For the circumcision on which they have trusted hath been done away; for he hath declared that circumcision was made not of the flesh. But they went out of the way, for an evil angel beguiled them. He saith unto them, "These things saith the Lord your God (so do I find the

commandment), Sow not upon thorns, be ye circumcised unto your Lord." And why saith he, "Be ye circumcised in the hardness of your hearts, and ye shall not be stiffnecked"? Take again, "Behold, saith the Lord, all the nations are uncircumcised with uncircumcision *of the flesh*, but this people is uncircumcised in their hearts." But thou wilt say, Yea, verily, the people hath been circumcised for a seal; but likewise is every Syrian and Arabian, and all the priests of idols: think ye they too are of their covenant? Moreover, the Egyptians also are in circumcision. Understand then, children of love, concerning all things richly, that Abraham, who first gave circumcision, circumcised looking forward in the spirit unto Jesus, having received the ordinances of three letters. For he saith, "And Abraham circumcised of his household eighteen males and three hundred." What then was the knowledge that was given unto him? Understand ye that he saith the eighteen first, and then, after an interval, three hundred. In the eighteen, I H, thou hast Jesus. And inasmuch as the cross was destined to show forth grace in the *sign* T, he adds three hundred. So then he showeth forth Jesus in the two letters, and in the single one the cross. He knoweth it who hath put within us the engrafted word of his doctrine; no man hath learned of me a truer instruction, but I know that ye are worthy.

10. [Spiritual significance of Moses's commands respecting various kinds of foods.]

11. Let us inquire whether it pleased the Lord to show beforehand of the water [of baptism] and of the cross. [Such references discerned in Jer. ii. 12, 13; Isa. xvi. 1, 2, xlv. 2, 3, xxxiii. 16–18; Ps. i. 3–6; Zeph. iii. 19; Ezek. xlvii. 12.]

12. Likewise again he giveth intimation concerning the cross in another prophet, saying: "And

when shall these things be accomplished? saith the Lord. When a tree is bent down and rises again, and when blood shall drop out of wood." Again thou hast *a testimony* of the cross and of Him that should be crucified. And he speaketh again in Moses, when the strange nations made war upon Israel; and that he might call to their remembrance in *the midst* of war that for their sins they were delivered unto death, the Spirit speaketh in the heart of Moses that he should make a type of the cross and of Him that should suffer, *showing*, saith he, that except they hope upon him they shall be at war for ever. So Moses put one shield upon another in the midst of the battle, and he stood above them all and stretched forth his hands; and so Israel again prevailed; then, as soon as he let down his hands, they were again smitten to death. To what end? that they might know that they can not be saved except they hope upon him. And again in another prophet he saith, "The whole day long have I spread out my hands to a people disobedient and gainsaying my righteous way." Again Moses setteth forth a type of Jesus, that he must suffer and that he shall make alive whom they shall think to have slain, by the sign of a pole when Israel was falling. For the Lord made all manner of serpents to bite them, and they died (for through the serpent was transgression found in Eve), that he might convince them, that for their transgression's sake they should be delivered unto the affliction of death. Yea, furthermore, though Moses himself gave commandment, "Ye shall have no molten nor graven image for your god," *yet* he himself made *it* that he might show forth a type of Jesus. Moses therefore made a serpent of brass, and put it up conspicuously, and called the people *together* by a proclamation. When they were come together therefore to the same *place*, they entreated Moses, that he should offer for their being made whole. But Moses spake unto them and said: When any man of you is bitten, let him come to the serpent that is set upon the wood, and let him hope *thereon*, believing that it is able even though dead to restore to life, and immediately he shall be saved. And they did so. In these things too thou findest again the glory of Jesus, that in him and unto him are all things. Again what saith Moses to Jesus (Joshua), the son of Nave, to whom he gave this name as being a prophet, that all the people might give ear *to him* only, because *in him* the Father makes all things manifest concerning his son Jesus? Moses then saith unto Jesus, son of Nave, when he gave him this name and sent him forth to spy out the land, "Take a book into thy hands, and write what the Lord saith, that the Son of God shall cut off by the roots all the house of Amalek at the last days." Behold again Jesus, not a son of man, but Son of God, by type manifested in the flesh. Now since *some* will say that Christ is David's son, David himself prophesieth, fearing and understanding the error of sinful men: "The Lord saith unto my Lord, Sit thou at my right hand until I make thy enemies thy footstool." And again Esaias likewise saith, "The Lord said unto Christ my Lord, whose right hand I have holden, that nations should give ear before him, and the strength of kings will I break in pieces." Behold how David calleth him Lord, and Son of God.

13. [Christians and not Jews are heirs of the covenant, as prefigured in the preference of Jacob to Esau and Ephraim to Manasseh; and proved in the promise that Abraham should be the father of uncircumcised nations.]

14. Yea, verily, but let us inquire of the covenant which he swore to the fathers to give to the people, whether he hath given it. He hath given

it; but they were not found worthy to receive it because of their sins. [How Moses received the tables written with the finger of God, but cast them down; and we received the covenant from the Lord himself who was manifested for this end. See Isa. xlii. 6, 7, xlix. 6, lxi. 1, 2.]

15. Further it hath been written concerning the sabbath also in the Ten Words, wherein *the Lord* spake to Moses on Mount Sinai face to face, "And keep ye the sabbath of the Lord holy with pure hands and a pure heart." And in another *place* he saith, "If my sons observe my sabbath, then will I cause my mercy to rest upon them." He speaks of the sabbath at the beginning of the creation: "And God made the works of his hands in six days, and made an end on the seventh day, and rested on it and sanctified it." Give heed, *my* children, why he saith thus, "He made an end in six days." This he saith, signifying that in six thousand years the Lord will make an end of all things; for one day is with him a thousand years. And he himself beareth me witness, saying, "Behold, to-day shall be as a thousand years." Therefore, *my* children, in six days, *that is to say* in six thousand years, shall an end be made of all things. "And he rested on the seventh day." This signifieth, *that* when his son shall come and utterly destroy this *present* time, and shall judge the ungodly, and change the sun, and the moon, and the stars, then he shall truly rest on the seventh day. Yea, and he saith furthermore, "Thou shalt keep it holy with pure hands and a pure heart." If, then, a man is now able to keep holy the day which God hath made holy, without being pure in heart, we have gone utterly astray. Behold then he doth *not* truly rest and keep it holy *until* that day when we shall ourselves be able so to do, having been justified and having received the promise, where

ungodliness is no more, but all things are made new by the Lord; then shall we be able to keep it holy, having been ourselves first made holy. Furthermore he saith unto them, "Your new moons and sabbaths I can not away with." Look ye how he saith, "Your present sabbaths *are* not acceptable unto me, but *the sabbath* which I have made, in the which, when I have finished all things, I will make the beginning of the eighth day, which is the beginning of the new world." Wherefore also we keep the eighth day unto gladness, in the which Jesus also rose from the dead, and, after that he had been manifested, ascended into the heavens.

16. [Concerning the true spiritual temple of God, that it is not a house made with hands, but the purified heart of the believer. The chapter contains these words:] Ye perceive that their (the Jews') hope is vain. Moreover, he again says, "Behold, they who have cast down this temple, even they shall build it up again." It has so happened. For through their going to war, it was destroyed by their enemies; and now they, as the servants of their enemies, shall rebuild it.

17. [All things in the present are thus explained. Should the author write about future things, the readers would not understand.]

---

18. But let us pass also to another *form of* knowledge and doctrine. There are two ways of doctrine and authority, the *way* of light and the *way* of darkness. And between these two ways there is a wide difference. For over the one are stationed light-bearing angels of God, but over the other angels of Satan. And *God* is the Lord from everlasting to everlasting, but *Satan* the prince of the time which now is of unrighteousness.

19. This then is the way of light, if a man desire to walk in the way toward the appointed place, and is zealous in his works. The knowledge then that hath been given us *whereby we may* walk therein is on this wise. [The principal virtues enumerated are to love God; to be simple in heart; to hate hypocrisy; to be lowly-minded; to be pure in heart and life; not to speak God's word amidst the unclean; not to respect persons; to be meek and peaceable; not to bear malice; not to take the Lord's name in vain; to love one's neighbor; not to commit murder by abortion; to train children in the fear of the Lord; not to be covetous; to bow before the visitations of God; to be obedient servants and kind masters; to be liberal; to love all who minister the word of the Lord; to remember the day of judgment; to seek daily the presence of saints; to labor to save souls; to hate the wicked; to judge justly; to make confession of sins; not to pray with an evil conscience.]

20. But the way of blackness is crooked and full of cursing. For it is a way of eternal death with punishment, wherein are those things which destroy men's souls—idolatry, insolence, haughtiness of power, hypocrisy, doubleness of heart, adultery, murder, extortion, pride, transgression, guile, malice, self-will, sorcery, witchcraft, covetousness, no fear *of God*. Persecutors *are they* of the good, hating truth, loving lies, knowing not the reward of righteousness, cleaving not to good, *cleaving* not to just judgment, heeding not the widow and orphan, watching not unto the fear of God but to evil, from whom meekness and patience *stand* afar off, loving vain things, pursuing after recompense, having no compassion on the poor, laboring not for him that is spent with labor, prone to evil speaking, knowing not Him that made them, slayers of children, defilers of God's workmanship, turning away

from him that is in need and oppressing him that is afflicted, advocates of the rich, lawless judges of the poor, filled with all manner of sin.

21. [Conclusion, in which exhortation is given to all obedience.] . . . For the day is at hand on which all things shall perish with the Evil One. The Lord is at hand and his reward. . . . Farewell, ye children of love and peace. The Lord of glory and of all grace be with your spirit, Amen.

AUTHORS OFTEN CLASSED

WITH

THE APOSTOLIC FATHERS.

HERMAS.

THE "Pilgrim's Progress of the Early Church" is the appropriate name given to the "Shepherd of Hermas." Who Hermas was—whether indeed there was a real character of that name who wrote the book, or whether, like *Christian*, it was a fictitious name—we do not certainly know. The earliest mention of the work is found in the Muratorian fragment on the canon, which says: "Hermas composed the Shepherd very lately in our times in the city of Rome, while the Bishop Pius, his brother, occupied the chair of the Roman Church; and it ought therefore indeed to be read, but it can never be publicly used in the church, either among the prophets [the number being complete], or the Apostles." A Latin poem ascribed to Pius gives a similar account. Irenæus quotes from the work with marked respect, and Clement of Alexandria refers to Hermas; but neither of them helps us to identify the author. Origen conjectures that he was the Hermas of Rom. xvi. 14—a guess doubtless prompted by the desire to give apostolic sanction to the book. For the "Shepherd" very soon came to be regarded as inspired, and as such was highly esteemed by most of the churches, though Tertullian speaks slightingly of it. In the absence of counter-evidence its authorship by Hermas, brother of Pius, may not unreasonably be accepted. This gives it a date from A. D. 130 to 140. The work is an allegory, now divided (though not by the manuscripts) into three parts—Visions, Commands, and Similitudes. Our text gives a large part of the book of visions, and sufficient from the other books to indicate their character. "The book," says Donaldson, "ought to derive a peculiar interest from its being the first work extant, the main effort of which is to direct the soul to God. The other religious books relate to internal workings in the church; this alone specially deals with the great change requisite to living to God. . . . Its creed is a very short and simple one. Its great object is to exhibit the morality implied in conversion."

The Sinaitic manuscript has given us an almost entire Greek text. There are, besides, Latin manuscripts not varying in substance from the Greek. The text here followed is the Greek as edited by Hilgenfeld.

THE SHEPHERD OF HERMAS.

[As now commonly edited, the "Shepherd" is divided into three books: I. Visions; II. Commandments; III. Similitudes.

Book One begins with Hermas's account of his

admiration for a beautiful lady, as he had rescued her from the river Tiber at Rome. Afterward, being alone in the country, praying, the spirit of this lady appears and reproaches him with an unhallowed regard for her, at which he is sadly grieved.

Vision First.—After the lady has disappeared, Hermas has a vision of an old woman clad in a splendid robe, and sitting in a great chair of wool, who charges him to admonish his household of their sins. She then reads to him from a book some very terrible words, closing, however, with words of gentleness. Rising up, her chair is borne away to the east by four young men, and she tells Hermas that the harsh words are for heathens and apostates, the mild ones for the righteous; after which two men bear her away to the east on their shoulders.

Vision Second.—Again, a year later, the same old woman appears to him and gives him a book to transcribe, which when he does, the book is snatched away by unseen hands. Soon after, the writing, at first unintelligible, becomes plain to him. It is a message relating principally to the faults of his wife and sons, but assuring him that he himself shall be saved on account of his simplicity and his great self-control, which traits shall save all who are characterized by them; it also contains a warning to one Maximus. Again, a revelation was made to Hermas while he slept, by a young man who explained that the old woman was the Church. Later this woman comes and directs him to prepare two copies of the book he had transcribed: one for Clement, who would send it to foreign countries; one for Grapte, who would admonish the widows and orphans. He himself was to "read the words in the city, along with the presbyters who preside over the church." Then follows vision third, which is here given entire.]

VISION THIRD.

1. The vision which I saw, my brethren, was of the following nature: Having fasted frequently, and having prayed to the Lord that he would show me the revelation which he promised to show me through that old woman, the same night the old woman appeared to me, and said to me, "Since you are so anxious and eager to know all things, go into the part of the country where you tarry; and about the fifth hour I shall appear unto you, and show you all that you ought to see." I asked her, saying, "Lady, into what part of the country?" "Wherever you will," said she. I chose a spot suitably retired. Before, however, I began to speak and to mention the place, she said to me, "I will come where you wish." Accordingly, brethren, I went to the country, and counted the hours, and reached the place where I had promised to meet her; and I see an ivory seat ready placed, and on the seat a linen cushion, and spread out above the linen a covering of fine linen. Seeing these laid out, and yet no one in the place, I began to feel awe, and as it were a trembling seized hold of me, and my hair stood on end, and a horror as it were came upon me, I being alone. But on coming back to myself and calling to mind the glory of God, I took courage, bent my knees, and again confessed my sins to God as I had done before. Whereupon the old woman approached, accompanied by six young men whom I had also seen before; and she stood behind me, and listened to me as I prayed and confessed my sins to the Lord. And touching me, she said, "Hermas, cease praying continually for your sins; pray for righteousness, that you may have a portion of it immediately

in your house." On this she took me by the hand, and brought me to the seat, and said to the young men, "Go and build." When the young men had gone and we were alone, she said to me, "Sit here." I say to her, "Lady, permit my elders to be seated first." "Do what I bid you," said she; "sit down." When I would have sat down on her right, she did not permit me, but with her hand beckoned to me to sit down on the left. While I was thinking about this, and feeling vexed that she did not let me sit on the right, she said, "Are you vexed, Hermas? The place to the right is for others who have already pleased God, and have suffered for his name's sake; and you have yet much to accomplish before you can sit with them. But abide as you now do in your simplicity, and you will sit with them, and with all who do their deeds and bear what they have borne."

2. "What have they borne?" said I. "Listen," said she; "scourges, prisons, great tribulations, crosses, wild beasts, for God's name's sake. On this account the right hand of the holy place is theirs, and every one's who shall suffer for God's name: the left hand is to the rest. But both for those who sit on the right and those who sit on the left there are the same gifts and promises; only those sit on the right and have some glory. You, then, are eager to sit on the right with them, but your shortcomings are many. But you will be cleansed from your shortcomings; and all who are not given to doubts shall be cleansed from all their iniquities up till this day." Saying this, she wished to go away. But, falling down at her feet, I begged her by the Lord that she would show me the vision which she had promised to show me. And then she again took hold of me by the hand, and raised me, and made me to sit on the seat to the left, and she sat down upon the right; and, lifting up a

splendid rod, she said to me, "Do you see something great?" And I say, "Lady, I see nothing." She said to me, "Lo! do you not see opposite to you a great tower, built upon the waters, of splendid square stones?" For the tower was built square by those six young men who had come with her. But myriads of men were carrying stones to it, some dragging them from the depths, others removing them from the land, and they handed them to these six young men. They were taking them and building; and those of the stones that were dragged out of the depths they placed in the building just as they were: for they were polished and fitted exactly into the other stones, and they became so united one with another that the lines of juncture could not be perceived. And in this way the building of the tower looked as if it were made out of one stone. Of those stones, however, which were taken from the dry land they rejected some, some they fitted into the building, and some they cut down and cast far away from the tower. Many other stones, however, lay around the tower, and the young men did not use them in building; for some of them were rough, others had cracks in them, others had been made too short, and others were white and round, but did not fit into the building of the tower. Moreover, I saw other stones thrown far away from the tower, and falling into the public road, yet not remaining on the road, but rolling into a pathless place; and others falling into the fire and burning; others also falling close to the water, and yet not capable of being rolled into the water, though they wished to be rolled down, and to enter the water.

3. On showing me these visions she wished to retire. I said to her, "Lady, what is the use of my having seen all this while I do not know what it means?" She said to me, "You cunning man,

wishing to know everything that relates to the tower." "Even so, O Lady," said I, "that I may tell it to my brethren, that, hearing this, they may know the Lord in much glory." And she said, "Many indeed shall hear, and hearing, some shall be glad and some shall weep. But even these, if they hear and repent, shall also rejoice. Hear, then, the parables of the tower; for I will reveal all to you. And give me no more trouble in regard to revelation, for these revelations have an end, for they have been completed. But you will not cease praying for revelations, for you are shameless. The tower which you see building is myself, the Church, who have appeared to you now and on the former occasion. Ask, then, whatever you like in regard to the tower, and I will reveal it to you, that you may rejoice with the saints." I said to her, "Lady, since you have once deemed me worthy of all being revealed to me, reveal it." She said to me, "Whatsoever ought to be revealed will be revealed; only let your heart be with God, and doubt not whatsoever you shall see." I asked her, "Why was the tower built upon the waters, O Lady?" She answered, "I told you before, and you still inquire carefully; therefore inquiring you shall find the truth. Hear then why the tower is built upon the waters: It is because your life has been and will be saved through water. For the tower was founded on the word of the almighty and glorious Name, and it is kept together by the invisible power of the Lord."

4. In reply I said to her, "This is magnificent and marvelous. But who are the six young men who are engaged in building?" And she said, "These are the holy angels of God, who were first created, and to whom the Lord handed over his whole creation, to exalt and build up and rule over every creature. By them will the building of the

tower be finished." "But who are the other persons who are engaged in carrying the stones?" "These also are holy angels of the Lord, but the former six are more excellent than these. The building of the tower then will be finished, and all will rejoice together around the tower, and they will glorify God because the tower is finished." I asked her, saying, "Lady, I should like to know what becomes of the stones, and what was meant by them." In reply she said to me, "Not because you are more deserving than all others that this revelation should be made to you—for there are others before you, and better than you, to whom these visions should have been revealed—but that the name of God may be glorified, has the revelation been made to you, and it will be made on account of the doubtful who ponder in their hearts whether these things will be or not. Tell them that all these things are true, and that none of them is beyond the truth. All of them are firm and sure, and established on a strong foundation.

5. "Hear now with regard to the stones which are in the building. Those square white stones which fitted exactly into each other are apostles, bishops, teachers, and deacons, who have lived in godly purity, and have acted as bishops and teachers and deacons chastely and reverently to the elect of God, some of them having fallen asleep, and some being still alive. And they have always agreed with each other, and been at peace among themselves, and listened to each other. On account of this, they join exactly into the building of the tower." "But who are the stones that were dragged from the depths, and which were laid into the building and fitted in with the rest of the stones previously laid?" "They are those who suffered for the Lord's sake." "But I wish to know, O Lady, who are the other stones who were carried from the

land." "Those," she said, "which go into the building without being polished are those whom God has approved of, for they walked in the straight ways of the Lord, and practiced his commandments." "But who are those who are in the act of being brought and placed in the building?" "They are those who are young in faith and are faithful. But they are admonished by the angels to do good, for no iniquity has been found in them." "Who, then, are those whom they rejected and cast away?" "These are they who have sinned and wish to repent. On this account they have not been thrown far from the tower, because they will yet be useful in the building if they repent. Those then who are to repent, if they do repent, will be strong in faith if they now repent while the tower is building. But if the building be finished, there will no longer be room, but they will be rejected. This [privilege] will only be theirs because they lie near the tower.

6. "As to those who were cut down and thrown far away from the tower, do you wish to know who they are? They are the sons of wickedness, and they believed in hypocrisy, and all iniquity did not depart from them. For this reason they are not saved, since they can not be used in the building on account of their iniquities. Wherefore they have been cut off and cast far away on account of the anger of the Lord, for they have roused him to anger. But as to the other stones which you saw lying in great numbers, and not going into the building, those which are rough are those who have known the truth and not remained in it, and have not been joined to the saints; on this account are they unfit for use." "Who are those that have rents?" "These are they who are at discord in their hearts one with another, and are not at peace among themselves; who indeed keep peace before

each other, but when they separate one from the other, their wicked thoughts remain in their hearts. These, then, are the rents which are in the stones. But those which are shortened are those who have indeed believed, and have the larger share of righteousness; yet they have also a considerable share of iniquity, and therefore they are shortened and not whole." "But who are these, Lady, that are white and round, and yet do not fit into the building of the tower?" She answered and said, "How long will you be foolish and stupid, and continue to put every kind of question and understand nothing? These are those who have faith indeed, but they have also the riches of this world. When, therefore, tribulation comes, on account of their riches and business they deny the Lord." I answered and said to her, "When, then, will they be useful for the building, Lady?" "When the riches that now seduce them have been circumscribed, then will they be of use to God. For as a round stone can not become square unless portions be cut off and cast away, so also those who are rich in this world can not be useful to the Lord unless their riches be cut down. Learn this first from your own case. When you were rich you were useless; but now you are useful and fit for life. Be ye useful to God, for you also will be used as one of these stones.

7. "Now, as to the other stones which you saw cast far away from the tower, and falling upon the public road and rolling from it into pathless places: they are those who have indeed believed, but through doubt have abandoned the true road. Thinking, then, that they could find a better, they wander and become wretched, and enter upon pathless places. But those which fell into the fire and were burned are those who have departed for ever from the living God; nor does the thought of

repentance ever come into their hearts, on account of their devotion to their lusts and to the crimes which they committed. Do you wish to know who are the others which fell near the waters, but could not be rolled into them? These are they who have heard the word, and wish to be baptized in the name of the Lord; but when the chastity demanded by the truth comes into their recollection, they draw back, and again walk after their own wicked desires." She finished her exposition of the tower. But I, shameless as I yet was, asked her, "Is repentance possible for all those stones which have been cast away and did not fit into the building of the tower, and will they yet have a place in the tower?" "Repentance," said she, "is yet possible, but in this tower they can not find a suitable place. But in another and much inferior place they will be laid, and that, too, only when they have been tortured and completed the days of their sins. And on this account will they be transferred, because they have partaken of the righteous Word. And then only will they be removed from their punishments when the thought of repenting of the evil deeds which they have done has come into their hearts. But if it does not come into their hearts, they will not be saved, on account of the hardness of their hearts."

8. When, then, I ceased asking in regard to all these matters, she said to me, "Do you wish to see anything else"? And as I was extremely eager to see something more, my countenance beamed with joy. She looked toward me with a smile and said, "Do you see seven women around the tower?" "I do, Lady," said I. "This tower," said she, "is supported by them according to the precept of the Lord. Listen now to their functions. The first of them, who is clasping her hands, is called Faith. Through her the elect of God are saved. Another,

who has her garment tucked up and acts with vigor, is called Self-restraint. She is the daughter of Faith. Whoever then follows her will become happy in his life, because he will restrain himself from all evil works, believing that, if he restrain himself from all evil desire, he will inherit eternal life." "But the others," said I, "O Lady, who are they?" And she said to me, "They are daughters of each other. One of them is called Simplicity, another Guilelessness, another Chastity, another Intelligence, another Love. When, then, you do all the works of their mother, you will be able to live." "I should like to know," said I, "O Lady, what power each of them possesses." "Hear," she said, "what power they have. Their powers are regulated by each other, and follow each other in the order of their birth. For from Faith arises Self-restraint; from Self-restraint, Simplicity; from Simplicity, Guilelessness; from Guilelessness, Chastity; from Chastity, Intelligence; and from Intelligence, Love. The deeds, then, of these are pure, and chaste, and divine. Whoever devotes himself to these, and is able to hold fast by their works, shall have his dwelling in the tower with the saints of God." Then I asked her in regard to the ages, if now there is the conclusion. She cried out with a loud voice, "Foolish man! do you not see the tower yet building? When the tower is finished and built, then comes the end; but it will be finished quickly. Ask me no more questions. Let this be a sufficient reminder and renewal of your spirits to you and to all the saints. But not for your own sake alone have these revelations been made to you, but that you may show them to all. For after three days—this you will take care to remember— I expressly command you, Hermas, to speak all the words which I am to say to you into the ears of the saints, that, hearing them and doing them, they may be cleansed from their iniquities, and you along with them.

9. "Give ear unto me, O Sons: I have brought you up in much simplicity, and guilelessness, and chastity, on account of the mercy of the Lord, who has dropped his righteousness down upon you, that ye may be made righteous and holy from all your iniquity and depravity; but you do not wish to rest from your iniquity. Now, therefore, listen to me and be at peace one with another, and visit each other, and bear each other's burdens; and do not partake abundantly of God's creatures alone, but give also of them to the needy. For some through the abundance of their food produce weakness in their flesh, and thus corrupt their flesh; while the flesh of others who have no food is corrupted, because they have not sufficient nourishment, and their bodies waste away. This intemperance in eating is thus injurious to you who have abundance, and do not distribute among those who are needy. Give heed to the judgment that is to come. Ye, therefore, who are high in position, seek out the hungry so long as the tower is not finished; for after the tower is finished you will wish to do good, but will find no opportunity. Give heed, therefore, ye who glory in your wealth, lest those who are needy should groan, and their groans should ascend to the Lord, and ye be shut out with all your goods beyond the gate of the tower. Wherefore I now say to you who preside over the church and love the first seats, Be not like to drug-mixers; for the drug-mixers carry their drugs in boxes, but ye carry your drug and poison in your heart. Ye are hardened, and do not wish to cleanse your hearts, and to mingle a purpose to do this with purity of heart, that you may have mercy from the great King. Take heed, therefore, children, that these dissensions of yours do not deprive you of

your life. How will you instruct the elect of the Lord if you yourselves have not instruction? Instruct each other, therefore, and be at peace among yourselves, that I also, standing joyful before your Father, may give an account of you all to your Lord."

10. On her ceasing to speak to me, those six young men who were engaged in building came and conveyed her to the tower, and other four lifted up the seat and carried it also to the tower. The faces of these last I did not see, for they were turned away from me. And as she was going, I asked her to reveal to me the meaning of the three forms in which she appeared to me. In reply she said to me: "With regard to them, you must ask another to reveal their meaning to you." For she had appeared to me, brethren, in the first vision the previous year under the form of an exceedingly old woman, sitting in a chair. In the second vision her face was youthful, but her skin and hair betokened age, and she stood while she spoke to me. She was also more joyful than on the first occasion. But in the third vision she was entirely youthful and exquisitely beautiful, except only that she had the hair of an old woman; but her face beamed with joy, and she sat on a seat. Now I was exceeding sad in regard to these appearances, desiring to know what the visions meant. Then I see the old woman in a vision of the night, saying: "Every prayer should be accompanied with humility; fast, therefore, and you will obtain from the Lord what you beg."

I fasted therefore for one day. That very night there appeared to me a young man, who said: "Why do you ask in prayer that revelations be granted you? Take heed lest by asking many things you injure your flesh. Be content with these revelations. Will you be able to see greater revelations than those which you have seen?" I answered and said to him: "Sir, one thing only I ask, that in regard to these three forms the revelation may be rendered complete." He answered me: "How long are ye sensitive? But your doubts make you sensitive, because you have not your heart turned toward the Lord." But I answered and said to him: "From you, sir, we shall learn these things more accurately."

11. "Hear, then," said he, "with regard to the three forms, concerning which you are inquiring. Why in the first vision did she appear as an old woman seated on a chair? Because your spirit is now old and withered up, and has lost its power in consequence of your infirmities and doubts. For, like elderly men who have no hope of renewing their strength and expect nothing but their last sleep, so you, weakened by worldly occupations, have given yourselves up to sloth, and have not cast your cares upon the Lord. Your spirit therefore is broken, and you have grown old in your sorrows." "I should like then to know, sir, why she sat on a chair." He answered: "Because every weak person sits on a chair on account of his weakness, that the weakness of his body may be sustained. Lo! you have the form of the first vision.

12. "Now in the second vision you saw her standing with a youthful countenance, and more joyful than before; still she had the skin and hair of an aged woman. Hear," said he, "this parable also. When one becomes somewhat old, he despairs of himself on account of his weakness and poverty, and looks forward to nothing but the last day of his life. Then suddenly an inheritance is left him; and hearing of this, he rises up, and becoming exceeding joyful, he puts on strength, and now no longer reclines, but stands up; and his

spirit, already destroyed by his previous actions, is renewed, and he no longer sits, but acts with vigor. So happened it with you on hearing the revelation which the Lord revealed to you. For He had compassion on you, and renewed your spirit, and ye laid aside your infirmities, and vigor arose within you, and ye grew strong in faith; and the Lord, seeing your strength, rejoiced. On this account he showed you the building of the tower; and he will show you other things if you continue at peace with each other with all your heart.

13. "Now, in the third vision, you saw her still younger, and she was noble and joyful, and her shape was beautiful. For just as when some good news comes suddenly to one who is sad, immediately he forgets his former sorrows, and looks for nothing else than the good news which he has heard, and for the future is made strong for good, and his spirit is renewed on account of the joy which he has received; so ye also have received the renewal of your spirits by seeing these good things. As to your seeing her sitting on a seat, that means that her position is one of strength, for a seat has four feet and stands firmly. For the world also is kept together by means of four elements. Those therefore who repent completely and with the whole heart will become young and firmly established. You now have the relation completely given you. Make no further demands for revelations. If anything ought to be revealed, it will be revealed to you."

[Two visions more close the book. *Vision Fourth.*—In this is seen a great beast, indicating the tribulations that are to come upon men. *Vision Fifth.*—To Hermas, lying upon his couch, appears one dressed like a shepherd, and announces himself as sent to be his guardian. He also directs Hermas to write down the commandments and similitudes which he makes known, and which are comprised in Books Two and Three.

[*Book Two.*—The twelve commandments are: 1. On faith in the One God; 2. On avoiding evil, and on giving alms in simplicity; 3. On avoiding falsehood, and on Hermas's repentance for his dissimulation; 4. On putting away one's wife for adultery; 5. Concerning anger and patience; 6. How to recognize the two spirits attendant on each man; 7. On fearing God and not the devil; 8. On shunning the evil and doing the good; 9. On praying with confidence; 10. Of grief as crushing out the Holy Spirit; 11. On trying the spirits by their works; 12. Of banishing every evil desire and putting on the good and holy desire.]

[*Book Three* is commonly divided into ten Similitudes, though several of the divisions contain no similes. *Sim. One*, which Bunsen would make part of the closing address of the previous book, enjoins upon Hermas, as upon one living in a foreign city, not to spend his wealth for earthly houses and lands, but to "buy afflicted souls," and minister to widows and orphans, and thus purchase houses and lands in his own city, against the day when he shall be called to reside in it. *Sim. Two* likens the elm and the vine, in their mutual dependence, to the rich man and the poor man; the rich supports the poor by his benefactions; the poor blesses the rich by his prayers. *Sim. Three* likens trees in the winter, when the green can not be distinguished from the withered, to men in this world, where the just can not be distinguished from the unjust. *Sim. Four* likens the summer of the year, when some trees are budding and fruiting and others appear withered, to the world to come, the "summer of the righteous," when the just will show fruit, but the heathen and sinners, those who have been occupied with overmuch business here, will appear withered and unfruitful. *Sim. Five*, under the figure of a slave, laboring faithfully in his master's vineyard, and receiving reward therefor by being associated as co-heir with the master's son, presents the Son of God. He, the Flesh in which dwelt the Holy Spirit, served faithfully here on earth, and is now received by God as co-heir and partner with the (unincarnate) Holy Spirit (the master's son). By this is taught the dignity of the body, which, as enshrining the Spirit, is to be· kept pure. Doing this will be a true fasting unto God. *Sim. Six*, under the figure of two shepherds, one gayly-clad and merry, dancing among his sheep, one clothed in goat-skin and austere, and treating his sheep harshly, represents the angel of luxury and deceit and the angel of punishment and penitence. The latter takes such as have given themselves up to luxury, but have not blasphemed the name of the Lord, and punishes them in this world, until they become true servants of the Lord. Those who have blasphemed the name of the Lord are left to death, there being for them no repentance. *Sim. Seven* contains no simile. They who repent must bring forth worthy fruits. *Sim. Eight* pictures a great willow-tree overshadowing plains and mountains, under which congregate all who have called on the name of the Lord, and receive from a majestic angel branches from the tree. These branches they afterward return, some wholly and some partially withered, some wholly green, some budding and fruiting. The angel crowns those with the fruitful branches, and sends them into the Tower. Those whose branches are variously withered are given over to the angel of penitence, who takes their branches and plants and waters them, so that some of them become green and even fruitful, after which they are again presented to the angel who had distributed them. This willow is God's law.

The branches are the law as received into the hearts of believers. Accordingly as these do or do not bring forth fruit, they are rewarded or are remanded to a course of discipline under God's care, until at last they receive of his grace and live. Only those who have blasphemed the Lord utterly perish. *Sim. Nine* is the most elaborate and beautiful of all. From a hill in Arcadia an angel shows to Hermas a vast plain with twelve mountains around, the first black as soot, the second without grass, the third full of thorns, the others becoming fruitful more and more to the twelfth, which is white and very beautiful. In the midst of the plain is a great white rock, higher than the mountains, capable of holding the whole world. The rock is old, but has a splendid gate appearing new. Around the gate are twelve virgins. Six distinguished-looking men summon a multitude and command that a tower be built above the rock, which is done, the virgins carrying the stones through the gate. Some of the stones are brought from the mountains, some are taken from the earth near by, and all alike, when placed in the tower, become beautifully white. The building finished, the Lord of the tower, in stature overtopping the tower, comes to inspect it. The imperfect stones are removed, and those suitable are redressed for other places. The rest are borne back to the mountains by twelve women, very beautiful in form, clothed in black, and with disheveled hair. The tower, completed, appears as one smooth stone. That night Hermas remains alone with the virgins by the tower, rejoicing and praying with them. The next day all is explained. The rock and the gate are the Son of God. The tower is the Church. The twelve virgins are Faith, Continence, Power, Patience, etc. The women in black are Unbelief, Incontinence, Disobedience, Deceit, etc. The mountains are the twelve nations inhabiting the world, who, however various, become one when joined together in the Church of God. *Sim. Ten* presents Hermas receiving commands concerning a ministry of repentance and almsgiving, which he is to perform with the help of twelve virgins (Christian virtues) who will abide with him.]

PAPIAS.

"Treasure held in earthen vessels" is the suggestion of a leading Christian scholar in referring to the gospel in the hands of Papias. But, however earth-born his own conceptions of gospel truth, he undoubtedly testifies as to the existence and the origin of two of our gospels. He was bishop of Hieropolis, a friend of Polycarp, and a hearer of many intimate acquaintances of the apostles, notably of Aristion and the presbyter John. His work suggests for him a Judaic origin, though he may have been a Phrygian. The approximate period of his life was A. D. 75–150. He wrote (*cir.* 130–140) a work in five books, "Expositions of Oracles of the Lord," of which only a few fragments are left. This is thought to have been a commentary on the gospels, though it is claimed by some to have treated only of our Lord's *words*, as handed down by tradition. Whatever it was, the illustrative matter was drawn from testimonies by the "living voice" of those who had talked with apostles. Among other informants, Papias mentions the daughters of Philip the Evangelist, who related that a dead man had been raised to life in his (probably Philip's) day, and that Justus Barsabas had drunk poison without harm. The most noticeable features of the work are its strong chiliasm and its gross literalism. There was to be "a certain millennium after the resurrection," and "a corporeal reign of Christ on this very earth." The work, says Eusebius, who had it entire, "used proofs from the First Epistle of John, and likewise from that of Peter." It is said by Andreas Cæsariensis to have testified to the inspiration of the Revelation. The estimates put upon Papias vary. Eusebius says he was learned in the Scriptures, but "very limited in his comprehension." Irenæus rates him much higher. Although more nearly contemporary with Justin, he is commonly associated with the Apostolic Fathers, as here. Hope is entertained that we may some time have more than these fragments, as a manuscript of Papias "On the Words of the Lord" was in existence as late as A. D. 1218.

FRAGMENTS FROM THE EXPOSITION OF ORACLES OF THE LORD.

From the Preface, as found in Eusebius, quoting Irenæus.

And I shall not be backward in subjoining to my interpretations whatsoever I at any time learned with accuracy from the elders, and remembered faithfully, affirming it to be true; for I have not, as do the many, found pleasure in those who say many things, but in those speaking the truth; nor in those treasuring up strange commands, but in those [mindful of] what was given from the Lord to the faith, and who proceed from the truth itself. But if indeed, anywhere, one who had followed the elders came, I inquired searchingly about the words of the elders—what Andrew or what Peter said, or what Philip, or what Thomas or James, or what John or Matthew; or which other of the Lord's disciples [had spoken] that which also Aristion and the presbyter John, disciples of the Lord, spoke. For that which I obtained from books seemed not so valuable to me as what [I derived] from the living and abiding voice.

[Eusebius also speaks of "a tradition which he (Papias) sets forth concerning Mark, who wrote the Gospel, in the following words:"]

And the presbyter said this: Mark, being the interpreter of Peter, wrote accurately whatever he remembered, though indeed not [setting down] in order what was said or done by Christ; for he did not hear the Lord, nor did he follow him: but afterward, as I said, [he followed] Peter, who adapted his discourses to the necessities of the occasion, but not so as to furnish a systematic account of the oracles of the Lord; so that Mark committed no fault when he wrote some things as he recollected them. For of one thing he took care—to pass by nothing which he heard and not to falsify in anything.

["Of Matthew," Eusebius continues, "he has stated as follows:"]

Matthew wrote the oracles in the Hebrew tongue; and every one interpreted them as he was able.

THE APOLOGISTS

OF THE

SECOND CENTURY.

The Age of the Apologists was the time when the rising faith first began to make formal expositions and defenses of itself before the learned world. Not all the works of the age were of this apologetic character; on the contrary, the range of Christian literature was now wide, in comparison with that of the earlier part of the period. Besides letters, such as those of Dionysius of Corinth, there were chronicles, like that of Hegesippus; books of tradition, like those of Papias; visions, such as the "Shepherd of Hermas"; tales, like the Clementine; treatises on particular doctrines, like that of Athenagoras on the resurrection; and other forms of composition.

Characteristic Writings.—Still the works which characterized the age were apologies, or treatises in defense either of Christians or of Christian truth. These were of two kinds: first, those addressed to political rulers, and designed to secure to Christians their political rights; secondly, those intended to influence individual opinions. The latter class may again be grouped as : 1, those directed to Gentile minds ; 2, those setting forth the claims of Christianity as against Judaism ; 3, those defending the faith against heretics. The remains of these writings are small, but sufficient to show us what they were.

Two of the earliest apologetic writers were the Athenians Quadratus and Aristides. Both their apologies were of the first class, having been addressed to the Emperor Hadrian during one of his visits to Athens. The appeal of Quadratus is said to have procured the rescript to Minucius in favor of the Christians. (See p. 180.) The single passage of this apology which we have is the following : "The works of our Saviour were always present; for they were real : even those healed and those raised from the dead : who were seen not only when they were healed and raised up, but also [were seen] continually, being present; and that not only while the Saviour remained, but also after his departure for a considerable time, so that some of them survived even to our time."

An apology of the second class, which, if not actually written at Athens, yet, judging from its tone, might have been, is the valuable "Epistle to Diognetus." It belongs to the group directed to gentile and philosophic thinkers. The second group of this class was represented by such works as the "Dialogue between Jason and Papiscus," which has been attributed to Aristo of Pella. This work, which was praised by Origen for its dramatic skill, represented a Hebrew Christian as convincing an Alexandrian Jew that the prophecies of the Messiah were applicable to Jesus. The third group contained works like that of Agrippa Castor. He wrote in refutation of Basilides, and, by certain strictures which he made upon the latter's use of imaginary prophets, proved to us that the second century was not wholly devoid of historical criticism.

Other apologies of the first class were those of Claudius Apollinaris, Miltiades, Melito, Justin, and Athenagoras. All of these writers addressed apologies to the Emperor Marcus Aurelius. The first, who was bishop of Hierapolis, wrote various treatises, of which we have left only two short fragments in regard to the observance of Easter. Of the works of Miltiades, who was a converted rhetorician, we have nothing. Of the other three, sketches are given before their several writings. Suffice it here to say that the central Christian figure and the representative apologist of his age was Justin. Two names only remain to be mentioned, of the apologists who adhered to the Catholic Church. Theophilus was made bishop of Antioch during the reign of Marcus Aurelius. Besides other works, he wrote (in the reign of Commodus) three books to Autolycus, which have come down to us. These books were designed to convince a learned heathen of the truth of Christianity, and are chiefly prized to-day on account of their many references to books of the New Testament. Hermias, of whom we know nothing save that he was called the philosopher, and lived toward the close of the period, wrote a brief work entitled "A Deriding of Gentile Philosophers."

An exceptional writer of his age was Hegesippus.

He was a Hebrew, who, desirous of learning the doctrines and practices of the whole Church, made a journey from Jerusalem to Rome, visiting many bishops on the way, and finding among all the same doctrine. The results of his inquiries he recorded in five "Memorials of Ecclesiastical Transactions." The books are now lost, but they were in the hands of Eusebius, who classes Hegesippus with other "champions of the truth" whose writings proved their orthodoxy and soundness in the faith. Some interest centers in this writer on account of the claim made by certain critics that he was an Ebionite, and that, since he says that all the churches of his day were agreed, the whole Church was strongly Judaistic down to a late day, when, by the influence of the forged Gospel of John, it was carried over to the Catholic doctrines. The simple reply made to this conjecture has been that Eusebius explicitly testified to Hegesippus's orthodoxy.

Dionysius of Corinth and Pinytus were mentioned in our introduction, as also a letter from the churches of Vienne and Lyons. This letter, preserved in large part by Eusebius, was written to the brethren in Asia and Phrygia, and gave a detailed account of the fearful torture and the triumphant faith of the Christians who had lately been persecuted. These Western churches also subjoined their opinions as to the Montanists, who were then first appearing in the East, which opinions, says Eusebius, were " at once pious and most orthodox."

Heretics.—An estimate of the Christian life of this age can not be rightly formed without considering certain writers outside the Church. From the days of the apostles there had been teachers of false doctrines, more or less closely associated with the great body afterward known as Catholic Christians. There were existing in the age under discussion two opposite types of error: Ebionism, or a heretical exaggeration of the Jewish-Christian idea of ritual observances; and a speculative Gnosticism, which dealt with Christianity as a philosophy rather than as a power to regenerate mankind. It was an age of intellectual activity, and, as we have seen, Christianity was beginning to displace the old philosophies. But with Christian truth there was mingled by the Gnostics every variety of Oriental theological and Greek philosophical speculation. Such views came to prevail very widely, side by side with Christian teachings, and thus controversies between Christians and Gnostics formed a feature of the religious life of the day.

Among Gnostic writers should be noticed Basilides, who lived early in the century. He claimed to have certain esoteric knowledge, given him by Matthias, who had heard it from the Lord when teaching privately. Origen says that he wrote a "gospel," which is now conjectured to have been a work on the philosophy of Christianity, or possibly commentaries on the Gospel. Later lived Valentinus, who gave his name to a Gnostic sect. He professed to follow the teachings of one Theodas, a follower of Paul. He wrote the "Gospel of Truth," a work thought to have been speculative and mystical, rather than historical like the canonical Gospels. Two other "gospels" of a similar character circulated among the Gnostics: the "Gospel of

Eve" and the "Gospel of Perfection." Heracleon and Ptolemæus were both Valentinians. The former wrote commentaries on the Gospels; the latter systematized the teachings of Valentinus. Of the works of these four writers only fragments are left; but these are regarded with interest, from their testimony to the early recognition of the New Testament books as Scripture.

We notice now two important heretical writers who were at one time connected with the Catholic Church. Tatian was a disciple of Justin, and carried on the latter's work at Rome for a little time after his death. Subsequently, removing to the East, he became leader of the Gnostic sect known as the Encratites. Tatian wrote many works, of which we have only one, an "Address to Greeks," written probably before he left the Church. He wrote also an important work known as the "Diatessaron," which Eusebius says was "a combination and collection of the Gospels," and which began with the opening statement of the Gospel of John.

Marcion, also contemporary with Justin, was a man of great personal power. He left the church after having, as it is said, aspired to the first place in the church at Rome, and gained in time a great following. Polycarp is said to have denounced him as the "first-born of Satan." His doctrine was of an extreme anti-Judaistic type, Pauline writings alone being received by him as Scripture. He formed the first canon of the New Testament, which consisted of "The Gospel," a recension of Luke, and "The Apostolicon," or ten epistles of Paul. Among other works written by Catholics against

Marcion were those of Philippus and Modestus, that of the latter being extant in the time of Jerome.

AUTHOR OF EPISTLE TO DIOGNETUS.

"Indisputably, after Scripture, the finest monument we know of sound Christian feeling, noble courage, and manly eloquence." Such is the estimate of this work by Bunsen, and yet of its author we *know* literally nothing. Long assigned without reason to Justin, the epistle has since been variously conjectured to be the work of Apollos, Quadratus, Aristides, and Marcion. Others, influenced by the absence of all allusions to the epistle in ancient writers, have called it a modern forgery. The author of "Supernatural Religion" thinks it a late work, "written expressly in imitation of early Christian feeling." Commonly, however, it is allowed to be an early work, the assigned dates ranging somewhere from A. D. 125 to 175. The epistle is in two parts—caps. i.-x. and xi.-xii.—of which the second is by a later (though not much later) author than the first. Part first has a distinctively Grecian cast, exalting *faith;* part second an Alexandrian tone, extolling *knowledge.* The whole work is claimed by apologists to bear strong testimony to the writings of John and Paul. The single original manuscript, from which the text here used was derived, was destroyed in 1870.

EPISTLE TO DIOGNETUS.

1. Since I see thee, most excellent Diognetus, very eager to learn the habits of worship of the Christians, and inquiring very wisely and carefully concerning them—by the worship of what God, and how adoring him, they all despise the world and make light of death, and neither receive the gods worshiped by the Greeks nor cherish the superstition of the Jews; also what sort of love they cherish for one another; and why then this new sort of fashion has come into the world now, and not long ago—I heartily approve this thy desire, and seek from God, who gives us to speak and to hear, both to grant me so to speak that above all thou, hearing, mayest be bettered, and to grant thee so to hear that I, speaking, shall not regret.

2. Come, then, having divested thyself of all the considerations preoccupying thy mind, and laying aside the habits which beguile thee, and becoming, as from the beginning, a new man, and as about to be a learner of a new doctrine, even as thou hast confessed, behold, not only with the eyes but also with the mind, of what nature or what form they happen to be whom ye think of and worship as gods. Is not one a stone, like that trodden upon; and another brass, not better than skewers wrought for our use; and another wood, even now rotten; and another silver, needing a man to guard it, that it may not be stolen; and another iron, weakened by rust; and another clay, no more sightly than that devoted to unhonored usage? Are not all these of perishable materials? Are they not forged by iron and fire? Did not the stone-cutter fashion one of them, and the brazier another, and the silversmith another, and the potter another? Before

they were wrought by the arts of these into these forms, had not each of them in its own way been transformed, as still happens? Would not what are now skewers, made of this material, should they chance upon the same artificers, become like to these? Are not these again which are now worshiped by you able to become skewers like the others by the power of man? Are they not deaf? Are they not blind? Are they not lifeless? Are they not without feeling? Are they not all liable to rot? Are they not all corruptible? Ye call these gods; ye serve them, ye worship them; and ye become absolutely like them. On account of this ye hate the Christians, because they do not deem these to be gods. [Why this?] For do not ye who now recognize and serve them much more cast contempt on them? Do ye not much rather mock and despise them, worshiping those of stone and clay without affording them keepers, and those of silver and gold, shutting up by night and placing under keepers by day, that they be not stolen? By that which ye intend to present to them as an honor, if they are sensible, ye rather punish them; but if they are senseless, ye convict them thereof when ye worship them with blood and the steam of sacrifices. Let one of you suffer these things. Let one of you endure that these things happen to himself. But no human being will willingly permit one of these affronts, for he has sensation and reason: the stone, however, permits it, for it is without sensation. Therefore do ye prove their want of sensation. Concerning the Christians not worshiping such gods, then, I am able to say many and different things; but if these should not seem sufficient to any one, I deem it superfluous to say more.

3. Next I deem thee most desirous of knowing about this, that they [Christians] do not worship

according to the same usages with the Jews. The Jews, then, if they avoid this servitude before mentioned, and if they deem it right to worship one God as Lord of all, think wisely; but if they offer this worship to him in a like manner with those before mentioned, they are foolish. For they, thinking to offer to God, as if he needed anything, those things, by the offering of which to the senseless and dumb the Greeks prove their folly, rightly declare it to be foolishness, not worship. For he, having made heaven and earth and all things in them, and providing for us all that which we need, himself has need of no one of those things which he supplies to those thinking to give. And those thinking to offer sacrifice to him with blood and smoke and burnt offering, and to honor him with these tokens, seem to me to differ in no way from those paying the same tribute to things that are dumb, that are not able to receive honor, in that they think to give something to one who has need of nothing.

4. But, in truth, as to their scrupulousness about meat, and the superstition about the sabbath, and the vain boasting of circumcision, and the hypocrisy about fasting and the new moon, ridiculous and not worthy of speech, I do not suppose you care to learn from me. For the receiving of some of the things created by God for the use of man as created well, and the rejection of some as useless and bad, how is it not godless? And the false representation of God as forbidding to do any good on the sabbath day, how is it not impious? And the pretending that the diminution of the flesh is a witness of election, as if on account of this they were especially beloved of God, how is it not worthy of ridicule? And their observance of months and days, being always with the stars and the moon, and their assigning of the appointments of God and the

changes of the seasons according to their own impulses, some for feasting and some for mourning, who thinks to be a proof of reverence to God and not much more of foolishness? I think thee, then, sufficiently persuaded that Christians rightfully abstain from the common vanity and error, and from the meddlesomeness and vain boasting of the Jews; but thou must not expect to be able to learn the mystery of their peculiar way of worshiping God from a man.

5. For Christians are different neither in country, nor speech, nor race, from the rest of men. For they do not anywhere inhabit a city of their own, nor do they use any strange dialect, nor do they follow any marked kind of life. This wisdom of theirs is not found out for them by any reflection or deep thought of inquisitive men, nor do they, like some men, set forth human doctrine. Inhabiting both Grecian and barbarian cities, as each has received by lot, and following the nations among whom they dwell in dress and food and the other affairs of life, they exhibit the wonderful and confessedly paradoxical character of their polity. They inhabit their native country, but only as sojourners; they share all things as citizens, and endure all things as foreigners; every foreign land is as their native country, and every land of their birth as a foreign land. They marry as do all, and beget children, but they do not expose their offspring; they have a common table, but not a common bed. They chance to be in the flesh, but they do not live according to the flesh; they reside upon earth, but their dwelling place is in heaven; they obey the established laws, and in their own lives they rise above the laws. They love all, and by all they are pursued. They are unknown, and are condemned; they are put to death, and are made alive again. They are poor, and they make

many rich; they are destitute of all things, and in all they abound. They are without honor, and in this want of honor they glory; they are evil spoken of, and they are justified. They are reviled, and they bless; they are insulted, and they pay honor. Doing good, they are punished as evil doers; being punished, they rejoice as being made alive. They are assailed by Jews as strangers, and by Greeks they are persecuted; and cause for the opposition those who hate them have none to assign.

6. But to put it plainly: As the soul is in the body, so are Christians in the world. The soul permeates all the members of the body, and Christians are throughout the cities of the world. The soul dwells in the body and is not of the body; Christians too dwell in the world and are not of the world. The soul, invisible, keeps guard in the visible body; and Christians are known as being in the world, but their way of worshiping God remains unseen. The flesh hates the spirit and makes war upon it, though suffering nothing, because it is prevented from enjoying pleasures; and the world hates Christians, being in no way injured, because they forswear pleasures. The soul loves the flesh which hates it, and the members; and Christians love those who hate them. The soul is shut up in the body, and itself preserves the body; Christians also dwell in the world as in a prison, and themselves preserve the world. The immortal soul abides in a mortal tabernacle; and Christians dwell in perishable [habitations], expecting incorruption in heaven. Deprived of food and drink, the soul becomes better; Christians again, punished every day, rather increase in numbers. To such a station God assigns them, which it were not lawful for them to forsake.

7. For this is not, as I say, an earthly invention which is committed to them, nor do they think it

worth their while to guard so carefully a mortal discovery, nor are they intrusted with the administration of human mysteries. But truly of his own accord the omnipotent and all-creating and unseen God himself fixed in men and established in their hearts the truth from heaven and the holy and incomprehensible Word; not, as some man might suppose [he would], having sent some servant, either messenger or governor, either one of those who direct earthly affairs, or one of those intrusted with governments in the heavens; but the very Creator and Fashioner of all things, by whom he confined the sea within its own bounds, whose mysterious laws all the starry signs faithfully observe, from whom the sun receives for observance the bounds of his daily course, whom the moon obeys as he commands to shine by night, whom the stars obey following in the course of the moon, by whom all things are marked out and defined and put in subjection, the heavens and things in the heavens, the earth and things in the earth, the sea and things in the sea, fire, air, the abyss, things in the heights and things in the depths, and those in middle space. This one he sent to them. Was it, then, as one might suppose, for tyranny and [to cause] fear and consternation? Not at all; but in 'sweet reasonableness' and mildness. As a King sending his son, a King, he sent him; as God he sent him; as to men he sent him; as saving he sent him; as persuading, not as compelling: for compulsion does not characterize God. He sent him as calling, not as pursuing us; he sent him as loving, not judging. For he will send him as judge; and who shall stand before his coming? .... [Dost thou not see them] thrown to the wild beasts in order that they may deny the Lord, and not overcome? Dost thou not see that as more of them are punished, so the rest increase the more? These things seem not to be the work of man; these are the power of God; these are the evidences of his manifestation.

8. For who among men at all understood what God is, until he came? Can it be that thou dost receive the senseless and frivolous words of those [deemed] trustworthy philosophers? of whom some said that God was fire (they call that God to which they are about to come), and some water, and some some other one of the elements created by God. And, indeed, if any one of these opinions is received, it would be possible also for each one of the other things created to be represented as God. But these things are the humbug and error of sorcerers. And no one of men has seen him or made him known; but he has revealed himself. And he has revealed himself through faith, by which alone it is permitted to see God. For God the Lord and Fashioner of all, having made all things, and having assigned them to their position, not only proved to be a lover of men, but also long-suffering. But he was always of such nature, and is and shall be, kind and good and without wrath and true, and he is alone good; and having considered the great and unspeakable plan, he communicated it to his Son alone. So long, therefore, as he kept in mystery and guarded his own wise counsel, he seemed to be unmindful and careless of us; but when he made a revelation through his beloved Son, and disclosed the things prepared from the beginning, all things came to us at once, both to share in his good deeds and to see and notice things which who of us would even have expected?

9. Having already therefore administered all things by himself with his Son, during [all] the time past, he suffered us as we would to be carried away with lawless impulses, being overcome of pleasures and lusts, not at all delighting in our sins, but suffering [them], neither approving of the then

time of unrighteousness, but working out the present [time] of righteousness; that being convinced in that time of our unworthiness of life through our own works, we might now become worthy through the goodness of God; and having made manifest the impossibility of coming through our own selves into the kingdom of God, we should become able through the power of God. And when our sin was filled up, and it was made fully manifest that the reward of the same, punishment and death, was expected, and the time came which God had already appointed to make manifest his goodness and power—O the surpassing benevolence and love of God!—he did not hate us, nor thrust us away, nor bear us malice; but he was long-suffering and forbearing. He himself took on him our sins, himself gave his own Son a ransom for us, the holy One for the lawless, the blameless One for the wicked, the righteous One for the unrighteous, the spotless One for the defiled, the immortal One for mortals. For what else but his righteousness was able to cover our sins? By whom could we, lawless and disobedient, be made righteous but by the Son of God alone? O sweet exchange! O untraceable working! O unexpected kindnesses! that the lawlessness of many should be hid in One who is righteous, and the righteousness of One should make righteous many who were lawless. Having then proved in the time past the powerlessness of our nature to attain to life, and having now made manifest a Saviour, able to save even things [which it was once] impossible to save, by both these things he sought that we should believe in his goodness; that we should esteem him our Nourisher, Father, Teacher, Counsellor, Healer, Wisdom, Light, Honor, Glory, Power, Life; that we should not be anxious about dress and food.

10..If thou also dost desire this faith, thou must

first gain a knowledge of the Father. For God loves men, on whose account he made the world, to whom he subjected all things in [the earth], to whom he gave reason, to whom understanding, to whom alone he gave to look upward to himself, whom he formed after his own image, to whom he sent his only begotten Son, to whom he gave promise of the kingdom in heaven, and he will give it to those who love him. And knowing [the Father], with what joy dost thou think to be filled? Or how wilt thou love him who has so loved thee before? And having loved, thou mayest be an imitator of his goodness. And do not wonder if it is possible for a man to be an imitator of God. If he desire it, it is possible. For it is not happiness, either to oppress one's neighbors, or to wish to have preëminence over those who are weaker, or to be wealthy and use violence toward inferiors; nor is any one able by these things to be an imitator of God, but these things are foreign to his majesty. But whoever takes upon himself the burdens of his neighbor, who, in whatsoever he is superior, wishes to benefit him who is lacking, who, whatever he has received from God, by ministering to those who lack becomes a God to them receiving, this one is an imitator of God. Then thou shalt see, being upon earth, that God rules in heaven; then shalt thou begin to speak the mysteries of God; then thou shalt both love and admire those who are punished on account of their unwillingness to deny God; then thou shalt condemn the deceit of the world and the error, when thou knowest what it is truly to live in heaven, when thou despisest what is here called death, when thou fearest what is truly death, which is reserved for those condemned to fire eternal which punishes those given over to it unto the end. Then those suffering for righteousness' sake the fire of the present thou shalt admire, and thou shalt deem them blessed when thou shalt know that fire . . . .

---

11. [I do not speak of strange things, nor do I seek things unlooked for; but, being a disciple of the apostles, I become a teacher of the Gentiles, ministering worthily of the things given me to those who are disciples of the truth. For who, having been rightly instructed, and having become a friend to the Word, does not seek to learn wisely the things made clearly manifest through the Word to the disciples, to whom the Word appearing has revealed them, speaking frankly, not understood by unbelievers, but speaking in detail to disciples, who being accounted faithful by Him know the mysteries of the Father. On account of which he sent the Word that he might be manifest to the world, who having been despised by the people [the Jews], and being preached by the apostles, is believed on by the Gentiles. This is he who was from the beginning, appearing now and being found old, and being everywhere born in the hearts of the saints. This is the everlasting One, who is to-day accounted the Son, through whom the Church is enriched, and grace spread abroad is increased in the saints, supplying understanding, revealing mysteries, announcing seasons, rejoicing over the faithful, being given to those who seek, by whom the vows of the faith are not broken, and the landmarks of the fathers are not removed. Then the fear of the law is chanted, and the grace of the prophets is known, and the faith of the gospel is established, and the tradition of the apostles is guarded, and the grace of the Church is exultant. Grieving not which grace, thou shalt know what things the Word discourses, through whom he will, when he pleases. For whatsoever things we are moved to declare with pains by

the will of the commanding Word, from love of the things disclosed to us, we become sharers with you.

12. Reading and listening to which things with attention, ye shall know what things God has prepared for those who rightly love [him], being made a paradise of delight bearing in themselves a fruitful, flourishing tree, and being adorned with all manner of fruits. For in this place is planted the tree of knowledge and the tree of life; but the [tree] of knowledge does not kill, though disobedience destroys. For not without significance are the writings that God from the beginning planted in the midst of paradise the tree of knowledge and the tree of life, through knowledge revealing life; which not using properly, they who were from the beginning were stripped naked through the deceit of the serpent. For there is no life without knowledge, nor is knowledge secure without true life. Wherefore each was planted a neighbor to the other. Perceiving the force of which, the apostle, blaming that knowledge which, without the commanding force of truth, influences life, says, "Knowledge puffeth up, but love edifieth." For thinking to know anything without knowledge which is true and is testified to by the life, one knows nothing; he is deceived by the serpent, not having loved life: but knowing with fear, and seeking life, one plants with hope, expecting fruit. Let your heart be knowledge and your life true wisdom, contained within. Bearing which tree and seizing its fruit, you will be gathering always that which is desired by God, which the serpent does not touch; neither is Eve [then] approached by deceit, nor corrupted, but, a virgin, is trusted; and salvation is set forth, and apostles are filled with understanding, and the passover of the Lord advances, and the tapers are gathered and placed in order, and the Word, teach-

ing the saints, rejoices, by whom the Father is glorified: to whom be glory for ever. Amen.]

JUSTIN.

Philosopher and Martyr are the distinguishing titles of this chief of the early apologists. He was born in Samaria, of Greek parents, somewhere about A. D. 100. Becoming an earnest seeker after God, as he tells us in his "Dialogue with Trypho," he studied with the various philosophical sects, hearing the most to commend among the Platonists. At last, finding the object of his search revealed in the prophetic writings, which pointed to God the Father of all and to Christ as the Son of God (see "Dialogue"), he became a Christian. His conversion, like that of Paul, was a call to proclaim to the world the knowledge of Christ; not like the apostle, by founding Churches, but by retaining his philosopher's dress and habits, and quietly teaching this new and divine philosophy to all seekers after truth. Like Paul, he felt himself a debtor to all men, of every race and rank in life, to teach them, as much as in him lay, of his new Master and of the way of salvation. We see him at Ephesus using all his knowledge of Scripture to persuade a little group of Jews to receive Jesus as the promised Christ. We hear him in his apologies to the Emperors not merely arguing as a philosopher for the toleration of Christians, but appealing personally to the sovereigns of the world to accept this faith in a crucified Lord. Again we see him in his work at Rome, commending the truth to all who congregated there from every nation, and denouncing the falsehoods of heretics like Marcion and Crescens. In such labors he passed his life, his reward being —again like Paul—a martyr's death at Rome, A. D. 163. An ancient "Martyrium" says that, in company with other confessors, he was beheaded.

Justin's praises are sounded by the whole early Church. Writers like Irenæus and Tertullian borrowed very largely from his works; later fathers appeal to him as to one speaking with authority; no other name so great as his intervenes between John and Origen. It is, however, the man more than his writings that we admire ; and in the writings it is the truth which he utters, rather than the form in which he puts it, that attracts us. He appears in the midst of that cultured and curious, but hollow and heartless second century, like an old Hebrew prophet waking after a sleep of centuries, and assuming the philosopher's cloak as the nearest approach to his old sheepskin mantle. He denounces woes upon the Cæsar if he does not repent, as boldly as Elijah rebuked the sins of Ahab. He feels through every fiber of his being that he is called to utter the truth of God, and so speaking he knows no fear. And yet, with all his prophetic boldness, Justin was a philosopher, and, in spite of of occasional narrow reasonings, he was a broad thinker. He could discern good beyond the circle of nominal believers in Christ. For his doctrine of the *Logos,* by which Christianity appeared to him as the full and perfect manifestation in humanity of that Divine Word or Reason of which philosophy and prophecy had already given feeble suggestions, led him to commend everything that was true in philosophy, as well as in prophecy, as of God. They who had uttered such truth were Christians. Socrates was a Christian; Elijah was a Christian. They were not, however, Christ. Some seeds of the λόγος σπερματικός had germinated within them. They were not themselves the Word that was God. Still, for what they were, Justin revered them. God had spoken through them. Suffering for the truth, they had been martyrs of the Word, as truly as any who were then witnessing with their lives. Thus the history of the world had been one continuous progress of the Divine Word, making himself felt somewhat among the Greeks, revealing himself more fully among the Hebrews, but at last standing forth in entirety in the Saviour of the world.

Justin's works, of the genuineness of which there is no reasonable doubt, are two "Apologies," addressed to the emperors, and the "Dialogue with Trypho." There are attributed to Justin, but on doubtful evidence, the following works: "An Address to the Greeks," "A Hortatory Address to the Greeks," fragments of a work on "The Resurrection of the Dead," and a work on the "Sole Government of God." Other works have been assigned to him which have no shadow of claim to his authorship.

A large part of the "First Apology" is here given. Of the "Dialogue," which, in full text, is of about the size of this volume, only a summary could be given—full enough, however, to indicate the scope and order of the argument.

THE FIRST APOLOGY OF JUSTIN.

1. To the Emperor Titus Ælius Adrianus Antoninus Pius Augustus Cæsar, to his son Verissimus the philosopher, and Lucius the philosopher, the natural son of Cæsar, but the adopted son of Pius, and the lover of learning, and to the sacred Senate, and to the whole people of Rome, in favor of those men of all nations who are unjustly hated and oppressed, I, Justin, the son of Priscus, and grandson of Bacchius, native of Flavia Neapolis, a city of Palestine, being one of them, have composed this address and petition.

2. Reason directs that all who are really pious and philosophical should honor and love that alone which is true, and refuse to follow the opinion of the ancients, should they prove to be worthless; for sound reason requires that we should not only reject those who do or teach anything wrong, but that by every means, and before his own life, the lover of truth ought, even if threatened with death, to choose to speak and to do what is right.

You everywhere, then, hear yourselves termed pious, and philosophers, and guardians of justice, and lovers of learning; it shall [now] be seen whether you are indeed such. For we have not come to flatter you by these writings of ours, nor to bespeak favor; but to make our claim to be judged after a strict and searching inquiry; so that neither by prejudice, nor desire of popularity from the superstitious, nor by any unthinking impulse of zeal, nor by that evil report which has so long kept possession of your minds, you may be urged to give a decision against yourselves. For it is our maxim that we can suffer harm from none, unless we be convicted as doers of evil, or proved to be wicked: you may indeed slay us, but hurt us you can not.

3. But lest any should think that this is a senseless and rash assertion, I entreat that the charges against us may be examined; and if they be substantiated, let us be punished as it is right to punish any other; but if no man has anything of which to accuse us, true reason does not allow you through a wicked report to wrong the innocent, or rather yourselves, who (so doing) are disposed to conduct this suit not by judgment but by passion. And every sober-minded person will think this to be the only good and right proceeding, namely, that the subjects should give a blameless account of their life and doctrine; and that their rulers should, on the other hand, equally give sentence, not under the guidance of violence and tyranny, but of piety and wisdom. Thus will both prince and people be blessed. For one of the ancients has somewhere said, "Unless the princes and people become philosophers, it is impossible for cities to become happy." It is my undertaking, then, to give all men an account both of our life and doctrines; lest, instead of those who see fit to be ignorant of our customs, we should pay the penalty of those offenses which they blindly commit; but it is your duty, as reason requires, when you hear us, to approve yourselves good judges. For if, for the rest, you, having understood, do not what is just, it is [an offense] without excuse against God.

4. The naming of a name, then, implies neither good nor evil, apart from the actions which are connected with that name; and we, as far as the name that is laid to our charge goes, must be considered as very good men. [Referring to the similarity of χριστός, Christ, and χρηστός, excellent.] But as we should not think it right, if convicted of any crime, to ask to be acquitted for the sake of the name, so on the other hand, if we be found guilty of no wrong, either through our adoption of a name

or through our mode of life, it is your duty to take anxious care that you do not, by unjustly punishing the innocent, justly bring punishment on yourselves. From a name, then, neither praise nor punishment can rightly spring, unless something be produced good or bad in practice. [The test must reach the lives of the individuals who bear the name.]

5. [The charge of atheism comes from demons who likewise accused Socrates.]

6. Hence it is that we are even termed atheists. And we confess ourselves atheists as regards such beings if they be esteemed as gods, but not with respect to the most true God and Father of righteousness and sobriety, and all other virtues, and who partakes not of evil; but both him and his son, who came from him, and taught us these truths, and the host of the other good angels who follow and imitate him, and the Spirit of prophecy, we reverence and worship, honoring him in reason and truth, and fully instructing every one who wishes to learn as we are taught ourselves.

7. [Each Christian must be tried by his own life.]

8. [Christians confess their faith in God, who, by Christ, will punish the wicked everlastingly.]

9. [Folly of idol worship.]

10. And we have learned that God has no need of material offerings from man, seeing that he gives us all things, and we have been taught, and are convinced and believe, that he only receives those who imitate the virtues which appertain to him, namely, temperance, and justice, humanity, and all that is worthy of a God who is called by no proper name. And we are also taught that he in his goodness created all things in the beginning from shapeless matter, for the sake of men, who, if by their works they approve themselves worthy to

his counsel, shall, we believe, be thought worthy of a dwelling with him, there to reign with him, free henceforth from corruption and suffering. For as he created us at first when we were not, so also we believe that he will hold those who choose what is pleasing to him worthy, because of their choice, of immortality and of dwelling with himself; for though our birth was not originally our own doing, yet in order that we may choose to follow what is pleasing to him, he, by the reasonable faculties which he has bestowed on us, both persuades us, and leads us to faith. And we think that it is to the benefit of all men that they are not prohibited from the knowledge of these things, but are even urged to turn their attention to them. For what human laws were incapable of doing, that the Word, which is divine, would effect, were it not that the evil demons, aided by the wicked and varied inclination to evil, which is in the nature of every man, have scattered about so many false and godless accusations, of which none apply to us.

11. And, when you hear that we look for a kingdom, you rashly conclude that we mean a human one, although we declare that it is to be that which is with God, as is proved by the fact that, when examined by you, we own ourselves to be Christians, though we know that for every one who confesses this the punishment is death. For, if we expected a human kingdom, we should deny our name that we might escape destruction, and should endeavor to elude you, that we might obtain our expectations; but since we fix not our hopes on the present, we take no thought when men murder us, death at any rate being owed by all.

12. [Christians live as under God's eye, and so should not be feared by good princes.]

13. That we are not atheists, therefore, what moderate person will not confess, from our worship

of the Creator of this universe, whom we assert, as we have been taught, to have no need of sacrifices of blood, and libations, and incense, but whom we praise to the best of our power with the reasonable service of prayer and thanksgiving, in all our oblations, having been instructed that the only service that is worthy of him is, not to consume by fire what he has given us for our sustenance, but to apply it to our own benefit, and to that of those who are in need, and, showing ourselves grateful to him, in speech to offer him solemn acts of worship and hymns for our creation, for all our means of health, for the qualities of things, and for the changes of seasons, and putting up prayers that we may have a resurrection to incorruptibility through our faith in him. Our Teacher of these things is Jesus Christ, who was even born for that purpose, and was crucified under Pontius Pilate, procurator of Judea in the reign of Tiberius Cæsar; whom, having learned him to be the Son of the very God, and holding him to be in the second place, and the Spirit of prophecy in the third, I will prove that we worship with reason. From this, however, people assure us of madness, affirming that we assign the second place, after the immutable and eternal God and Father of all things, to a crucified man; not knowing the mystery that is herein; to which I entreat you to give heed, as I proceed to explain it.

14. [The demons misrepresent Christian doctrine.]

15. On chastity then he [Christ] spoke thus: "Whosoever looketh upon a woman to lust after her, hath committed adultery with her already in his heart before God." And, "If thy right eye offend thee, pluck it out; it is better for thee to enter into the kingdom of heaven with one eye, rather than having two eyes to be cast into everlasting fire." And, "Whosoever shall marry her that

is divorced from another husband, committeth adultery." And, "There are some who are made eunuchs of men, and some who are born eunuchs, and some who have made themselves eunuchs for the kingdom of heaven's sake; but all can not receive this saying." So that all who, by human law, contract second marriages, are sinners in the eyes of our Master, and they who look upon a woman to lust after her; for not only is the man who commits adultery in fact rejected by him, but even he who does so in will, since not only are our works manifest to God, but even our very wishes. And there are many men and women, of sixty and seventy years of age, who were disciplined to Christ from their youth, and now remain spotless; and it is my pride to be able to produce such from every nation. What shall I say, too, of that countless multitude who have laid aside their former licentiousness, and learned these things? For Christ called not the righteous and the temperate to repentance, but the wicked and the intemperate, and the unjust. And he spoke as follows; "I came not to call the righteous, but sinners, to repentance." For our heavenly Father would rather the repentance of a sinner than his punishment.

And, on the love that we should bear to all men, he taught thus: "If ye love them which love you, what new thing do ye? For even fornicators do the same. But I say unto you, Pray for your enemies, love those that hate you, bless them which curse you, and pray for them which despitefully use you." And to incite us to communicate to those who have need, and to do nothing for praise, he said: "Give to every one that asketh, and from him that would borrow turn not away; for if ye lend to them of whom ye hope to receive again, what new thing do ye? This even the publicans do. Lay not up for yourselves treasures upon earth where moth and rust doth corrupt, and where thieves break through; but lay up for yourselves treasures in heaven, where moth and rust doth not corrupt. For what is a man profited, if he shall gain the whole world and lose his own soul; or, what shall a man give in exchange for it? Lay up for yourselves therefore treasures in heaven, where neither moth nor rust doth corrupt." And, " Be you kind and merciful, as your Father is kind and merciful, who maketh his sun to rise upon sinners, on the just and on the evil. Take no thought what ye shall eat, or what ye shall put on. Are ye not much better than birds and beasts? And yet God feedeth them. Be not therefore solicitous what ye shall eat, or wherewithal ye shall be clothed; for your Father which is in heaven knoweth that ye have need of these things. But seek ye first the kingdom of heaven, and all these things shall be added unto you. For where the treasure is, there also is the mind of man." And, " Do not these things to be seen of men, otherwise ye have no reward of your Father which is in heaven."

16. And what he said about being patient and ready to assist all men, and free from anger, is as follows: " Whosoever shall smite thee on thy cheek, turn to him the other also; and him that would take away thy cloak or thy coat, forbid not. Whosoever is angry is in danger of the fire. Whosoever shall compel thee to go a mile, go with him twain. Let your good works so shine before men, that they may see them, and glorify your father which is in heaven." For we ought not to rise up in strife, nor would he have us imitators of the wicked, but he has urged us, by patience and meekness, to convert all from shame and the lust of evil. And this [work] I have to show in the case of many that were numbered with you, who changed from violent and tyrannical characters, being overcome either

from having watched the constancy of their neighbors' lives, or from having observed the wonderful patience of fellow travelers under unjust exactions, or from the trial they made of those with whom they were concerned in business.

And with regard to not swearing at all, and always speaking the truth, he has commanded as follows: "Swear not at all; But let your yea be yea, and your nay, nay; for whatsoever is more than these is of evil." And he thus persuaded us that it is right to worship God alone. "This is the greatest commandment, Thou shalt worship the Lord thy God, and him only shalt thou serve, with all thy heart, and with all thy strength, the Lord thy God which made thee." And when one came to him and said, "Good Master," he answered saying, "There is none good but God only, who made all things." But let those who are not found to be living as he commanded be assured, that they are not Christians at all; even though with the tongue they confess the doctrine of Christ; for he has declared that not the sayers only, but those who are also doers, shall be saved. His words are as follows: "Not every one that saith unto me, Lord, Lord, shall enter into the kingdom of heaven, but he that doeth the will of my father which is in heaven: for whosoever heareth me, and doeth what I say, heareth him that sent me. For many will say unto me, Lord, Lord, have we not eaten and drunk in thy name, and done wonders? And then will I say unto them, Depart from me, ye that work iniquity. Then shall there be wailing and gnashing of teeth, when the righteous shall shine forth as the sun, but the wicked are sent into everlasting fire. For many shall come in my name, clothed outwardly in sheep's clothing, but inwardly they are ravening wolves; ye shall know them by their works. But every tree that bringeth not forth good fruit is hewn down, and cast into the fire." And we entreat that they who are not living according to his commandments, but who are only called Christians, may be punished also by you.

17. We everywhere, before all things, endeavor to pay tribute and taxes to those whom you appoint, as we were taught by him. For persons at that time came to him and asked him if it were lawful to pay tribute to Cæsar; and he answered: "Tell me whose image this coin bears? and they said, Cæsar's. And he answered them again, Render therefore unto Cæsar the things which are Cæsar's, and unto God the things that are God's." Hence we render worship to God alone, but we serve you gladly in other things, acknowledging you to be kings and rulers of men, and praying that you may be found to unite to your imperial power, sound wisdom also. But if you disregard our prayers and public professions, we shall suffer no loss, since we believe—I should rather say, we are fully convinced—that each will suffer punishment by eternal fire, according to the merit of his actions; and that an account will be required of every one in proportion to the powers which he received from God, as Christ has declared in these words: "For unto whomsoever God hath given much, of him shall the more be required."

18. For look back to the end of each of the Emperors, how they died the death which is common to all, which, if it terminated in insensibility, would be a godsend to all the wicked. But since sensation remains in all men who have been in existence, and everlasting punishment is in store, do not hesitate to be convinced and believe that these things are true. And, indeed, let even necromancy, and the divinations by uncontaminated children, and the invocation of human souls, and those who are termed by the magicians senders of dreams and

familiars, together with the actions of those who are acquainted with these things, persuade you that souls are in a state of sensation even after death; and those who are seized and dashed down by the souls of the dead, whom all term demoniacs, and insane, and your oracles as you term them, of Amphilochus, Dodona, Pytho, and others of the same kind, with the doctrine of your writers Empedocles and Pythagoras, Plato and Socrates, and the ditch of Homer, and the descent of Ulysses to see these [souls], and the testimony of these who have taught the same as these: in a like manner with [your reception of] whom, do you also receive us; for we believe in God no less than they, but more, for we expect to receive our bodies again, even after they are dead and cast into the earth, affirming that with God nothing is impossible.

19. [Possibility of the resurrection argued from the formation of the body from the human soul; containing also the following:] For we know that our Master Jesus Christ has said, "What is impossible with men is possible with God"; And "Fear not them that kill you, and after that have no power to do anything," he said, "but fear him who after he hath killed is able to cast both soul and body into Gehenna." This Gehenna is a place where all will be punished who live unrighteously, and who believe not that what God has taught through Christ will come to pass.

20. And the Sibyl, and Hystaspes, have said that there should be a dissolution of things corruptible by fire. And those philosophers who are termed Stoics teach that God himself shall be resolved into fire, and say that again, after this change, the world shall be formed anew; but we know that God, the Creator of all things, is superior to the things that are to be changed. If therefore we assert on certain points things like those poets

and philosophers whom you honor, but speak on others more convincingly and divinely than they, and if we only have proof, why are we thus unjustly hated beyond all? For in our assertion that all things were ordered and created by God, we are found to speak the language of Plato, and in our opinion that there will be a conflagration, we use that of the Stoics; but in our doctrine that the souls of the wicked will be punished, and are in a state of sensation after death, while those of the righteous are freed from torment and remain in bliss, we teach like the poets and philosophers. In denying that we ought to worship the work of men's hands, we agree with Menander the comedian, and others of his opinion; for they have said that the workman is greater than his work.

21. [Analogies to the history of Christ in what is believed of certain of the gods.]

22. But the Son of God, who is called Jesus, even if only a man in common with others, is worthy for his wisdom of being called the Son of God: for all your writers term God the Father both of men and of gods. And if we affirm that the Word of God was begotten of God even in a peculiar manner, and beyond the ordinary generation, as I have already said, let this be common to you who affirm Hermes to be the messenger-word from God. And should any object that he [Christ] was crucified, the fact is that this was also common to the forementioned sons of Jupiter of yours, who underwent suffering. For in their case the sufferings of death are not recorded to have been similar, but different; so that he appears not to be behind them even in his peculiar manner of suffering; nay, I will prove him superior, as I have undertaken to do in the previous part of my defense; or rather it is already proved; for he who is the superior shows it by his actions. But if we affirm that he was born of a

virgin, you also may take this as held in common of Perseus. And when we declare that he made the lame, paralytic, and blind from their birth whole, and that he raised the dead to life, even the like actions to those which are said to have been done by Æsculapius may we be thought to assert of him.

23. And that this also may be made plain to you (1), that whatever things we assert, having learnt them from Christ and the prophets who preceded him, are alone true, and more ancient than all writers; and that not because we say the same as they, we claim to be believed, but because we state the truth; and (2), [that] Jesus Christ alone is properly the Son of God, as being his Word and First-begotten, and Power, and that being made man by his will, he taught us these doctrines for the renewal and restoration of mankind; and (3), [that] before he was born as a man among men, certain men, at the instigation of the before-mentioned demons, by the instrumentality of the poets, recounted as facts what they [really] spoke as myth-makers, in the same way as they have fabricated the charges of impious and abominable deeds that are brought against us, and of which they have neither witness nor proof—I shall produce the following arguments.

24. [First, Christians alone are persecuted for the name of Christ, while others may worship every variety of gods.]

25. [Secondly, Christians have abandoned these false gods.]

26. Thirdly, after the ascension of Christ into heaven, the devils put forward certain men who styled themselves gods, who not only were not persecuted by you, but were even deemed worthy of honors. There was Simon of Samaria, a native of a village called Gitto, who in the time of Claudius Cæsar, through the craft of the devils working by

his means, performed acts of magic, and was held in your royal city of Rome to be a god, and was honored by you with a statue like a god, which statue was raised on the river Tiber, between the two bridges, bearing this inscription in the Roman language, "To Simon the holy god." And almost all the natives of Samaria, with a few of other nations, confessing him to be the first god, worship him; and a certain Helena, who traveled about with him at that time, and had formerly exposed herself in the stews, they term the first idea generated from him. I know, too, that one Menander, another Samaritan of the village of Capparatea, and a disciple of Simon, was also influenced by devils, and when in Antioch he deceived many by means of his magic; and he even persuaded his followers that they should never die, which some of his disciples still believe. And there is a Marcion of Pontus, who is even now teaching his disciples to believe in another and greater god than the Creator; who, by the assistance of devils, has made many of every nation utter blasphemies, denying the Creator of this universe to be God, and causing them to confess another, who as being a greater god has done greater things than he. All who come of these are, as I have said, called Christians; just as those who do not agree with the philosophers in their doctrines, yet bear the common title which is derived from philosophy. Whether or not these people commit those shameful and fabulous actions — the putting out the lights, indulging in promiscuous intercourse, and eating human flesh I know not; but that they are not persecuted and put to death by you, at least for their opinions, I do know. I have by me, however, a treatise composed against all the heresies that have existed, which, if you wish to peruse it, I will present to you.

27. [Wickedness and sad results of exposing children.]

28. For with us the prince of the evil spirits is called a serpent, and Satan, and the devil, as you may learn even from an examination of our writings; who, Christ has foretold, will be sent into fire with his host, and the men who are his followers, there to be tormented to an endless eternity. For the delay of God in not yet having brought this to pass is for the sake of the human race; for he foreknows that some will be saved by repentance, some even that are not yet perhaps born. In the beginning indeed he made man with understanding, and with the power of choosing the truth, and of acting uprightly, in order that all men might be without excuse before him, for they were created with reason and contemplation. If, therefore, any one shall not believe that God regards these things, or conclude indirectly that he has no existence, or affirm that he is, but takes pleasure in evil, or that he resembles a stone, and that neither virtue nor vice is anything, but men consider them to be good or bad in opinion only, this is the greatest impiety and injustice.

29. And again [we are taught not to expose children] lest any one of them may not be found, but may perish, and we be homicides. But we either do not marry at first, unless to bring up children; or, declining it, we live in continence. And to prove to you that promiscuous connection is not a mystery of ours, one of our number presented a petition to Felix, the Prefect of Alexandria, to entreat permission to be made an eunuch by a surgeon; for, without the sanction of that officer, the surgeons of the place said that they were prohibited from performing the operation. And when Felix would by no means consent to sign his petition, the young man remained single, and was satisfied with

his own conscience, and the conscience of those who were of the same mind with himself. And I do not think it irrelevant to allude in this place even to Antinoüs, who is lately dead, whom all were eager with fear to worship as a god, although they knew both who he was and what was his origin.

30. But lest any should ask us, in objection, what prevents him whom we call Christ from being a man, of men, who performed what we term miracles by magic craft, and therefore appeared to be the Son of God, I will now offer my proof, not trusting to the words of those who affirm these things, but necessarily believing those who foretold what should happen before it came to pass; for we see with our very eyes that events have happened, and are happening, as was foretold; and this will, I think, appear even to you the greatest and truest proof.

31. There were then certain persons among the Jews, who were prophets of God, by whom the Spirit of prophecy foretold events that were about to happen, before they came to pass; and the prophecies of these persons the King of Judah for the time being acquired and took care of, as they were spoken, when uttered prophetically in their own Hebrew language, and arranged in books by the prophets themselves. But when Ptolemy, King of Egypt, was forming his library, and endeavoring to collect the works of every author, he heard also about these prophetic writings, and sent to Herod, who was then King of the Jews, entreating that the books of the prophecies might be transmitted to him. And Herod the king sent them written in their Hebrew language mentioned before. But when their contents were not understood by the Egyptians, he sent a second time to request the presence of persons to translate them into Greek. When this was done, the books remained in the possession

of the Egyptians even to the present time, and they are in the hands of all the Jews throughout the world; who, although reading them, do not understand what is said in them, but consider us as their enemies and opponents, killing and ill-treating us, as you do, whenever they have the power, as you may well believe: for even in the late Jewish war, Barcochebas, the ringleader of the Jewish revolt, commanded that Christians alone should be dragged to cruel torture, unless they would deny Jesus to be Christ and blaspheme him. And we find it foretold in the books of the prophets that Jesus our Christ should come, born of a virgin, and grow to manhood, and heal every disease and every malady, and raise the dead, and be envied and unrecognized and crucified, and should die, and rise again and go up to heaven, and should both be, and be called, the Son of God; and that certain persons should be sent by him into every nation of men to proclaim these facts, and that rather the men of Gentile race should believe in him. And this was foretold be'ore his coming; at first, five thousand years; then, three thousand; then, two thousand; then, one thousand; and, lastly, eight hundred; for, according to the succession of generations, other and yet other prophets arose.

32. Moses then, in truth, who was the first of the prophets, spoke in these very words: "The scepter shall not depart from Judah nor a lawgiver from between his feet, until he come for whom it is in store; and he shall be the desire of the nations, binding his foal to the vine, and washing his robe in the blood of the grape." It is your duty to inquire with accuracy and learn until whose time there was a ruler and king among the Jews peculiar to themselves. [This was] until the appearance of Jesus Christ our Teacher, and the Expounder of those prophecies which were unknown, as was fore-

told by the divine and holy spirit of prophecy through Moses: "The scepter shall not depart from Judah, until he come for whom the kingdom is in store." For Judah was the forefather of the Jews, and it is from him that they derive the title of Jews; and you, since his (Christ's) appearance, have ruled also over the Jews, and held possession of their whole country. But the words, "He shall be the expectation of the Gentiles," signify that men from all nations should look for his coming again, as you yourselves may see and be convinced by the facts: for from all nations men look for him who was crucified in Judea, after whom the land of the Jews was at once delivered into your hands as a spoil of war. And the expression, "Binding his foal to the vine, and washing his robe in the blood of the grape," was a symbol significative of the events that were to happen to Christ, and of the works that should be performed by him. For the foal of an ass stood at the entrance of a village bound to a vine, and he commanded his disciples to bring it to him; and when it was brought, he mounted and sat upon it, and entered into Jerusalem, where was the chief temple of the Jews, which was subsequently destroyed by you; and after this he was crucified, that the rest of the prophecy might be fulfilled. For the words "Washing his robe in the blood of the grape" were prophetical of the passion which he was to undergo, cleansing by his blood those who believed on him. For that which the Divine Spirit terms by the prophet his robe are those who believe in him, in whom dwells that seed which is from God, namely, the Word. And what is called the blood of the grape, signifies that he who should appear would have blood, but not of human seed, but of Divine power. For the first Power after God the Father and Lord of all things, even his Son, is the Word, who took flesh and was made man, in the manner which shall be described hereafter. For as man made not the blood of the grape, but God, so also this blood is declared to have been not of human seed, but of the power of God, as aforesaid. And Isaiah, also another prophet, declaring the same things in other words, speaks thus: "A star shall rise out of Jacob, and a flower shall grow out of the root of Jesse; and in his arm shall the nations trust." A star of light has arisen, and a flower has sprung up from the root of Jesse, this the Christ. For of a virgin who was of the seed of Jacob the father of Judah, whom we have shown to be the father of the Jews, through the power of God was he born, and Jesse was his forefather according to this prophecy, and he was the son of Jacob and Judah, according to the succession of generation.

33. And again, hear how he was foretold in express terms by Isaiah, as about to be born of a virgin. It is spoken thus: "Behold, a virgin shall conceive, and bear a son, and they shall say of his name, God with us." For the things that are considered to be incredible and impossible with men, the same has God declared beforehand by the Spirit of prophecy to be about to come to pass; that when they have come to pass, they should not be disbelieved, but from having been foretold should be believed. But lest any, not understanding the prophecy which I have cited, should accuse us of saying the same things as we have laid to the charge of the poets, who say that for the sake of sensual gratifications Jupiter formed a union with women, I will endeavor to explain its expressions. The words then, "Behold, a virgin shall conceive," signify that the virgin shall conceive without intercourse. For, if she had intercourse with any one whomsoever, she was no longer a virgin; but the power of God coming upon the virgin overshad-

owed her, and caused her, being a virgin, to conceive. And the angel of God, who was sent to this same virgin at that time, brought her good tidings, saying, "Behold, thou shalt conceive in thy womb of the Holy Ghost, and shalt bring forth a Son, and he shall be called the Son of the Most High; and thou shalt call his name Jesus, for he shall save his people from their sins," as they who have related all the things about our Saviour Jesus Christ taught; whom we believe, for by the forementioned Isaiah also the Spirit of prophecy declared that he should be born as I have previously stated. It is right then to conceive the Spirit, and the power which is from God, to be nothing other than the Word, who is also the first-born of God, as Moses the forementioned prophet has declared. And this, when it came upon the virgin and overshadowed her, not by intercourse, but by power, made her pregnant. But the name Jesus in the Hebrew language means Σωτήρ (Saviour) in the Greek. Hence also the angel said to the virgin, "And thou shalt call his name Jesus, for he shall save his people from their sins." But that the prophets are inspired by no other than the Divine Word even you, as I think, will admit.

34. And hear in what part of the world he was to be born, as another prophet, Micah, declared. And thus he spoke: "And thou, Bethlehem, in the land of Judah, art not the least among the princes of Judah, for out of thee shall come forth a Governor, who shall feed my people." Now this is a certain village in the country of the Jews, thirty-five stadia distant from Jerusalem, in which Jesus Christ was born; as you may also learn from the lists of the taxing, which was made in the time of Cyrenius, the first governor of yours in Judea.

35. And that Christ, after his birth, should be unknown to other men until he was grown to man's

estate, which also came to pass, hear what was foretold of this. The words are as follows: "A child is born to us, and a young man is given to us, whose government is upon his shoulders," which is significant of the power of the cross; to which, when crucified, he applied his shoulders, as shall be shown more clearly in the course of my explanation. And again the same prophet Isaiah, who was inspired by the prophetical Spirit, says: "I have stretched out my hands to a disobedient and gainsaying people, to those who walk in a way that is not good. They ask me now for judgment, and presume to draw nigh to God." And again in other words, by another prophet, he says: "They pierced my hands and my feet, and cast lots upon my garments." Yet David, the king and prophet, who uttered these words, underwent none of these things; but Jesus Christ stretched out his hands, and was crucified by the Jews, who contradicted him and denied him to be the Christ. For, indeed, as the prophet said, they mocked him, and set him on the judgment-seat, and said, Judge us. But the words, "They pierced my hands and my feet," are a description of the nails that were fixed in his hands and his feet on the cross. And after he was crucified, those who crucified him cast lots for his garments and divided them among themselves. And that these things were so, you may learn from the Acts which were recorded under Pontius Pilate. And that he was expressly foretold as about to enter into Jerusalem, sitting on the foal of an ass, I will prove by the words of the prophecy of another prophet, Zephaniah. They are these: "Rejoice greatly, O daughter of Zion; proclaim it, O daughter of Jerusalem; behold thy King cometh to thee lowly, and riding upon an ass, and upon a colt the foal of an ass."

36. But when you hear the words of the proph-

ets spoken as by some person, you should not suppose them to be spoken by those who are inspired, but by that Divine Word who moves them. For at one time he declares as it were prophetically what is to come to pass; at another, he speaks as from the person of God, the Lord and Father of all things; at another, as from the person of Christ; at another, as from the person of the people answering the Lord or his Father; such as you may see even in your own writers, some one person being the writer of the whole, but introducing the persons who speak. This the Jews, who have the writings of the prophets, not understanding, acknowledged not Christ even when he came; but even hate us who affirm that he has come, and who prove that as was foretold he was crucified by them.

37. [Utterances of the Father. Citations from Isa. i. 3, 4; lxvi. 1; i. 11–15; lviii. 6.]

38. [Utterances of the Son. Citations from Isa. lxv. 2; l. 6; Ps. xxii. 16, 18; iii. 5; xxii. 7.]

39. But when, as prophesying what is about to come to pass, the Holy Ghost speaks, his words are as follows: "For out of Zion shall go forth the law, and the word of the Lord from Jerusalem. And he shall judge among the nations, and shall rebuke many people; and they shall beat their swords into plowshares, and their spears into pruning-hooks; and nation shall not lift up sword against nation, neither shall they learn war any more." And that it so came to pass you may believe. For from Jerusalem there went out into the world twelve men in number, and they obscure persons, and unskilled in speaking; but through the power of God they declared to every race of men that they were sent by Christ to teach all men the word of God; and we, who were formerly murderers of each other, not only make no war on our enemies, but, to avoid

even lying or deceiving those who examine us, we willingly confess Christ and die. For it were possible that what is said,

"My tongue has sworn it, but my mind's unsworn,"

we should do in this case. For it would be ridiculous that the soldiers who are mustered and enrolled by you should prefer even to their own life, their parents, their country, and all their kindred, their allegiance to you, although you are unable to give them any incorruptible reward; but that we, enamored of incorruptibility, should not endure all things, in order to receive the rewards we long for, from him who is able to give them.

40. Hear also how it was foretold of those who preached his doctrine and proclaimed his appearance, the beforementioned prophet and king speaking thus by the Spirit of prophecy: "Day unto day uttereth speech, and night unto night showeth knowledge. There is no speech nor language where their voices are not heard. Their voice has gone out through all the earth, their words to the end of the world. In the sun hath he placed his tabernacle, and he as a bridegroom that goeth out of his chamber shall rejoice as a giant to run his way." Besides these, I think it right and applicable to mention some other prophecies which were uttered by the same David, from which you may learn how the Spirit of prophecy urges men to live, and how he spake of that conspiracy of Herod the King of the Jews, and of the Jews themselves, and of Pilate your procurator in their country, with his soldiers, against Christ, and that men from every nation should believe in him, and that God calls him his Son, and has declared that he will put all enemies under him; and how the devils, as far as they can, endeavor to escape the power of God the Father and Lord of all, and that of Christ himself;

and how God calls all men to repentance before the day of judgment comes. He speaks thus: [quotation of the first and second psalms].

41. And again, in another prophecy, the same Spirit of prophecy, declaring through the same David that after his crucifixion Christ should reign, spoke as follows: [citation of Ps. xcvi., closing with the words, " The Lord hath reigned from the tree," the last three of which Justin (" Dial. Tryph.") accuses the Jews of having erased from the text].

42. But when the Spirit of prophecy speaks of what is about to happen as having already come to pass, as may be seen even from the passages previously cited by me, in order that this may not afford any excuse to my readers, I will explain this also. The things that are assuredly known by him as about to take place, he foretells as having already been fulfilled. And that we ought thus to receive it, consider with earnest application of mind what is uttered. David spoke the before-mentioned passages about fifteen hundred years before Christ was incarnate and crucified; and no one of those who were before his time, by being crucified, brought joy to the Gentiles; nor did any of those who were after him. But our Jesus Christ, being crucified and dying, rose again, and reigned, ascending into heaven; and, from the tidings which were proclaimed by him through the apostles in all nations, is the joy of those who look for the incorruptibility which is promised by him.

43. [Men, unlike irrational creatures, are free and responsible.]

44. [Having cited Deut. xxx. 15, 19, and Isa. i. 16–20, to prove that the prophets recognized men's responsibility, he says:] So also Plato, in his words, " The blame is his who chooses, but God is without blame," took his saying from Moses the prophet. For Moses was before all the writers of Greece.

And in all that both philosophers and poets have said about the immortality of the soul, or the punishments after death, or the contemplation of celestial subjects, and the like doctrines, they have taken their suggestions from the prophets, so as to be able to understand and explain those matters. Hence with all there appear to be seeds of truth, but they are proved to have understood them inaccurately, when they speak in contradiction of themselves. So that when we say that future events have been foretold, we do not assert that they came to pass by any compulsion of destiny, but that God, foreknowing what all men would do, and determining with himself that every man should be rewarded according to the worth of his actions, foretells by the Spirit of prophecy that men should receive even from him recompense in proportion to the worth of their works; always urging the human race to renewed exertion and recollection, and showing that he has a care of it, and takes thought for it. But through the agency of evil demons death was proclaimed against those who read the books of Hystaspes, or the Sibyl, or the prophets, that they might through fear turn their readers from receiving the knowledge of good, and keep them slaves to themselves; which in the end they were not able to accomplish. For we not only read them without fear, but also, as you see, offer them to you for inspection; knowing that they will appear well-pleasing to all. And if we convince even a few, we shall gain the greatest rewards, for, like good husbandmen, we shall receive the recompense from the Lord.

45. That God the Father of all things would bring Christ to heaven, after he rose from the dead, and keep him there until he smote the demons his enemies, and the number of those who are foreknown by him as being good and full of virtue should be accomplished, for whom he delays the

consummation, hear the words of the prophet David. They are as follows: [citation of Ps. cx. 1-3]. The words then, "He will send to thee the rod of power out of Jerusalem," are presignificant of that powerful doctrine which his apostles went out from Jerusalem and preached everywhere; and, although death is decreed against those who teach, or in any way confess, the name of Christ, we everywhere both embrace and teach it. And if you also should read these words as enemies, you can do no more, as I have already said, than put us to death, which to us indeed involves no loss, but to you, and to all who persecute us unjustly, and do not repent, brings eternal punishment by fire.

46. But lest any should unreasonably urge, to turn men away from our doctrines, that we assert Christ to have been born one hundred and fifty years ago, under Cyrenius, and to have taught under Pontius Pilate what we long afterward affirm that he did teach; and should urge it against us as if all men who were born before him were irresponsible, I will, by anticipation, answer this difficulty. We are taught that Christ is the first-born of God, and we have shown above that he is the Word, of whom the whole human race are partakers. And those who lived according to reason are Christians, even though accounted atheists, such as, among the Greeks, Socrates and Heraclitus and those who resembled them, and of the barbarians Abraham, and Ananias, and Azarias, and Misael, and Elias, and many others, from going through the list of whose actions or names, knowing that it would be tedious, I now beg to be excused. So also they who have been before him and lived without reason were worthless, and enemies to Christ, and murderers of those who governed their lives by reason; but they who lived and now live in accordance with it are Christians, and are fearless and tranquil. But for

what reason, through the power of the Word, according to the will of God, the Father and Lord of all things, he was born as man of a virgin, and was called Jesus, and was crucified, and died, and rose again, and went up into heaven, from all that I have said already at such length, a man of understanding will be able to comprehend. But as the discussion of the proof is not necessary now, I will pass on, for the present, to those proofs which are pressing.

47. That the land of the Jews, then, was to be laid waste, hear what was said by the Spirit of prophecy. His words were uttered as in the person of the people wondering at what had been done. They are as follows: [citation of Is. lxiv. 10–12]. And that Jerusalem was laid waste, as it was foretold should come to pass, you know. Of this desolation, and of none of its people being permitted to inhabit it, the prophet Isaiah spoke thus: "Their country is desolate, their enemies devour it in their presence, and there shall not be one of them to dwell in it"; and that it is guarded by you to prevent any one from dwelling in it, and that death is decreed against a Jew who is detected in entering it, you know well.

48. And that it was foretold that our Christ should heal all diseases, and raise the dead, hear what was said. It is as follows: [citation of Isa. xxxv. 5, 6.]. That he performed these things you may easily be satisfied, from the Acts of Pontius Pilate. And how it was foretold by the Spirit of prophecy that both he and those who trusted in him should lose their lives, hear what was said by Isaiah. It is this: [Isa. lvii. 1, 2].

49. And again, [hear] how it was said by the same Isaiah that the people of the Gentiles who did not look for him should worship him, but that the Jews who were always looking for him should not ac-

knowledge him when he came. His words were spoken as in the person of Christ himself. They are these: [quotation of Isa. lxv. 1-3]. For the Jews who had the prophecies, and always looked for Christ to come, knew him not; and not only so, but even ill-treated him; while the Gentiles, who never heard any thing about Christ until the apostles went out from Jerusalem, and preached the things concerning him, and gave them the prophecies, were filled with joy and faith, and put away their idols, and dedicated themselves to the unbegotten God, through Christ. But that these infamous things which were to be spoken against those who confess Christ were foreknown, and that they who slandered him, and who said that it was well to keep the ancient customs, were to be miserable, hear what is briefly said by Isaiah. It is this: "Woe unto those who call sweet bitter and bitter sweet."

50. But that when he had become man for our sakes, he endured to suffer and be dishonored, and that he shall come again with glory, hear the prophecies which were uttered on this subject. They are as follows: [quotation of Isa. liii. 12; lii. 13-15; liii. 1-8]. After his crucifixion, then, even they that were acquainted with him all denied and forsook him; but afterward, when he rose from the dead, and was seen by them, and taught them to read the prophecies in which all these things were foretold as about to happen, and when they had seen him go up into heaven, and had believed, and received power from thence, which was sent them from him, they went forth to the whole race of men, and taught these things, and received the name of apostles.

51. And further, to bear witness to us that he who suffered those things had a generation that could not be declared, and is King over his enemies, the Spirit of prophecy spoke thus: [quotation of

Isa. liii. 8 to end]. And hear how he was to go up into heaven as was prophesied. It was spoken thus: [citation of Ps. xxiv. 7, 8]. And how he was to come again from heaven in glory, hear what was said to this purport by the prophet Jeremiah. His words are as follows: "Behold, one like the Son of man cometh upon the clouds of heaven, and his angels with him."

52. [Certain fulfillment of the prophecy of a second advent of Christ. Citations from Ezek. xxxvii. 7; Isa. xlv. 23; lxvi. 24; Zech. ii. 6; xii. 11; Joel ii. 13; Isa. lxiii. 17; lxiv. 11.]

53. [Summary of the prophecies: Judea to be desolated; Gentiles to be converted, more in numbers than the Jews. Quotations of Isa. liv. 1; i. 9; Jer. ix. 26.]

54. [Heathen mythology arose from an imperfect imitation by demons of the truths of prophecy, they thinking thereby to prejudice men against the story of Christ. Citations of Gen. xlix. 10, 11; Ps. xix. 5.]

55. But in no case, and upon none of those who are called the sons of Jupiter, did they imitate the being crucified; for it did not occur to them, everything which was spoken in relation to this having been uttered symbolically, as I have already said. This, as the prophet foretold, is the greatest mark of his strength and power, as is also shown by the things which fall under our observation; for consider all the things in the world, whether without this form there is any administration, or any community possible to be maintained. The sea can not be plowed except that trophy which is called a sail abide safe in the ship; the earth is not tilled without it; diggers, handicraftsmen also, do not perform their task unless by tools bearing this shape. And the figure of man differs from that of the unreasoning brutes only in this, that he is up-

right, and has power to stretch out his hands; and has in his face extended from his forehead what is called his nose, through which the animal draws his breath, and which displays nothing else than the figure of the cross. And it is thus spoken by the prophet: "The breath before our face is Christ the Lord." And your symbols, those upon the banners and trophies with which your processions are universally made, display the power of this form; and by these you show the signs of your rule and authority, even if you do so without knowing what you do. And you consecrate the images of your emperors, on their demise, by this form; and by inscription you term them gods. And since we have urged you as far as our power admits, by reason, and this conspicuous figure, we know that henceforth we are blameless, even if you believe not; for our part is now done and perfected.

56. [Demons still mislead men through pretenders like Simon.]

57. [They cause us to be persecuted.]

58. [They also raise up heretics like Marcion.]

59. And that you may learn that Plato borrowed from our teachers (I mean the account which is given by the prophets) when he said that God altered shapeless matter, and created the world, hear how the same things are expressly taught by Moses, who has been mentioned before as the first Prophet, and older than the Greek writers, by whom the Spirit of prophecy, declaring how, and from what, God in the beginning created the world, spoke thus: "In the beginning God created the heavens and the earth. And the earth was invisible and unfurnished, and darkness was upon the face of the deep; and the spirit of God moved over the waters. And God said: Let there be light; and it was so." So that both Plato, and those who agree with him, and we ourselves, have learned, and you may be persuaded, that

by the Word of God the whole world was created out of substance which was described before by Moses. That too which the poets call Erebus, we know to have been previously mentioned by Moses.

60. So that which is spoken physiologically by Plato in his Timæus about the son of God, when he says "He placed him in the universe after the manner of the letter χ," he likewise borrowed from Moses. For it is related in the Mosaic writings that at the same time when the Israelites went out of Egypt, and were in the desert, venomous beasts, vipers, and asps, and every kind of serpents, assailed them, and destroyed the people; on which Moses, from the inspiration and direction communicated from God, took brass, and formed it into the shape of a cross, and placed it on the holy tabernacle, and said to the people, "If you look upon that figure and believe, you shall be saved." And when this was done, he related that the serpents died, and recorded that by this means the people escaped death.

Plato, then, read this: and not accurately knowing or perceiving that it was a figure of the cross, but seeing only the form of the letter χ, he said that the power next to the first God was in the universe in the shape of an χ. And his mention of a third is derived, as I have already said, from his reading the words of Moses, "The Spirit of God moved above the waters." For he gives the second place to the Word of God, who, he says, is placed after the manner of an χ in the universe, and the third to the Spirit who is said to move above the water, saying, "The third about the third." And hear how the prophetic Spirit declared by Moses that there should be a conflagration. He spoke as follows: "An everlasting fire shall descend, and burn to the pit below." It is not then that we hold the same opinion as others, but that all men imitate and repeat ours. For you may hear and learn these things among us, from those who do not even know the shape of their letters, but who are ignorant and rude in speech, though wise and faithful in mind, some too being blind or deprived of their eyes: thus you may perceive that these things have not been by human wisdom, but are uttered by the power of God.

61. How we dedicated ourselves to God, being new made through Christ, I will explain, lest, if I omit this, I appear to be cheating in my explanation. All, then, who are persuaded and believe that the things who are taught and affirmed by us are true; and who promise to be able to live accordingly, are taught to pray, and beg God with fasting to grant them forgiveness of their former sins; and we pray and fast with them. Then we bring them where there is water, and after the same manner of regeneration in which we also were regenerated ourselves, they are regenerated: for, in the name of God, the Father and Lord of all things, and of our Saviour Jesus Christ, and of the Holy Ghost, they then receive the washing of water. For Christ indeed said: " Except ye born again, ye shall not enter into the kingdom of heaven." And that it is impossible for those who are once born to enter into their mother's wombs, is plain to all. And it is declared by the prophet Isaiah, as I have already written, in what way those who have sinned, and who repent, shall escape their sins. It is said as follows: [quotation of Isa. i. 16–20]. And we have received the following reason from the apostles for so doing. Since we were ignorant of our first birth, and were born by necessity of the moist seed through the mutual union of our parents, and were brought up in evil customs and wicked training; in order that we might not remain the children of necessity and ignorance, but of choice and of knowl-

edge, and that we might obtain remission of the sins we had formerly committed: in the water there is called over him who chooses the new birth and repents of his sins, the name of God the Father and Lord of all things, and calling him by this name alone, we bring the person to be washed to the laver. For no one can declare the name of the ineffable God, but if any one presume to say that he has any, he commits an act of incurable madness. Now this washing is called illumination, because they who learn the meaning of these things are enlightened in their mind. And in the name of Jesus Christ, who was crucified under Pontius Pilate, and in the name of the Holy Ghost, who foretold by the prophets all these things about Jesus, does he who is enlightened receive his washing.

62. And the devils, hearing of this baptism which was taught by the prophet, instigate those who enter into their temples, and who are about to come before them, paying drink offerings and burnt offerings, also to sprinkle themselves; and they cause men to go and wash their whole persons before they come to the temples where they are enshrined. Moreover, the command given by the priests to those who enter the temples and worship in them to put off their shoes the devils have learned and imitated from what happened to Moses, the prophet whom I have mentioned. For at the time when Moses was commanded to go down into Egypt, and bring out the people of Israel who were there, as he was feeding the sheep of his uncle on the mother's side in the land of Arabia, our Christ held converse with him in the shape of fire from a bush, and said, " Put off thy shoes and draw near and hear." And when he put off his shoes and drew near, he heard that he was to go down into Egypt, and bring out the people of Israel who were there. And he re-

ceived a mighty power from Christ, who spoke to him in the shape of fire, and he went down and led out the people, having wrought great and wonderful things; which if you wish, you may learn them accurately from his writings.

63. But all the Jews teach even now that the unnamed God spoke with Moses; whence the Spirit of prophecy, when blaming them by Isaiah, the before-mentioned prophet, spoke as I have already related: "The ox knoweth his owner, and the ass his master's crib, but Israel doth not know me, my people hath not understood me." And Jesus the Christ, because the Jews knew not what the Father was and what the Son, upbraids them in like manner, and says: "No man knoweth the Father but the Son, nor the Son but the Father, and those to whom the Son will reveal him." But the Word of God is his Son, as I have already said. And he is called Angel and Apostle, for he declares all that ought to be known, and is sent to proclaim what is told, as indeed our Lord himself said: "He that heareth me heareth him that sent me." And this will be clear from the writings of Moses, in which it is said as follows: "And the Angel of God spake unto Moses in a flame of fire out of the midst of a bush, and said, I AM THAT I AM, the God of Abraham, the God of Isaac, and the God of Jacob, the God of thy fathers. Go down into Egypt, and bring up my people." And what followed you who wish may learn from them, for it is not possible to write all the events in this book. But thus much has been said to prove that Jesus, the Christ, is the Son and Apostle of God, being formerly the Word; and appearing at one time in the form of fire and at another in the image of incorporeal beings; but now, by the will of God, being made man for the human race. He endured also to suffer all that the devils caused to be inflicted on him by the senseless

Jews. Who, having it expressly said in the Mosaic writings, "And the Angel of God spake with Moses in a flame of fire in the bush, and said, I AM THAT I AM, the God of Abraham, the God of Isaac, and the God of Jacob," affirms that it was the Father and Maker of all things who spoke thus. Hence also the Spirit of prophecy upbraids them as follows: "Israel hath not known me, my people hath not understood me." And again, Jesus, as we have shown, when with them, said, "No one knoweth the Father but the Son, nor the Son but the Father, and those to whom the Son will reveal him." The Jews then, always thinking that the Father of all things spoke to Moses, he who spoke to him being the Son of God, who is called both Angel and Apostle, are rightly upbraided both by the Spirit of prophecy and by Christ himself, as knowing neither the Father nor the Son. For they who say that the Son is the Father are proved neither to know the Father, nor that the Father of all things has a Son, who, being moreover the first-born Word of God, is also God. And formerly, through the shape of fire, and through an incorporeal image, he appeared to Moses and the other prophets; but now, in the time of your government, as I said before, he was made man of a virgin, according to the counsel of the Father, for the salvation of those who believed on him, and endured to be set at nought and to suffer, that by dying and rising again he might overcome death. But that which was spoken from the bush to Moses, "I AM THAT I AM, the God of Abraham, the God of Isaac, the God of Jacob, and the God of thy fathers," is significant that they though dead remain in existence, and are the men of this very Christ; for these are the first of all men who were employed in the search after God, Abraham the father of Isaac, and Isaac the father of Jacob, as Moses also wrote.

64. And that the devils incited them to place the image of her who is called Proserpine at the fountains of waters, in imitation of what was spoken by Moses, you may perceive from what has been already said. For Moses declared, as I have previously written, " In the beginning God created the heavens and the earth; and the earth was invisible and unformed, and the Spirit of God moved upon the waters." In imitation then of the Spirit of God, which was said to be borne upon the water, they declared that Proserpine was the daughter of Jupiter. Minerva, too, in like manner, they craftily affirmed to be the daughter of Jupiter, not from sexual union; but when they knew that God, by his Word, conceived and made the world, they described Minerva as the first conception : which we consider to be most ridiculous, to adduce the female form as the image of the conception. And in like manner their actions convict the others who are called sons of Jupiter.

65. But after thus washing him who has professed, and given his assent, we bring him to those who are called brethren, where they are assembled together to offer prayers in common both for ourselves and for the person who has received illumination, and all others everywhere, with all our hearts, that we might be vouchsafed, now we have learnt the truth, by our works also to be found good citizens and keepers of the commandments, that we may obtain everlasting salvation. We salute one another with a kiss when we have concluded the prayers. Then is brought to the president of the brethren bread and a cup of water and wine, which he receives, and offers up praise and glory to the Father of all things, through the name of his Son and of the Holy Ghost, and he returns thanks at length for our being vouchsafed these things by him; when he has concluded the prayers and

thanksgivings, all the people who are present express their assent by saying Amen. This word, Amen, means in the Hebrew language, so let it be. And when the president has celebrated the eucharist, and all the people have assented, they whom we call deacons give to each of those who are present a portion of the eucharistic bread, and wine and water, and carry them to those who are absent.

66. And the food is called by us eucharist, of which no one is allowed to partake but he who believes the truth of our doctrines, and who has been washed with the washing that is for the forgiveness of sins and to regeneration, and who so lives as Christ has directed. For we do not receive them as ordinary food or ordinary drink; but as by the word of God Jesus Christ our Saviour was made flesh, and took upon him both flesh and blood for our salvation, so also the food which was blessed by the prayer of the word which proceeded from him, and from which our flesh and blood, by transmutation, receive nourishment, is, we are taught, both the flesh and blood of that Jesus who was made flesh. For the apostles, in the records which they made, and which are called gospels, have thus delivered to us what was commanded them; that Jesus took bread, and gave thanks, and said, "This do in remembrance of me: this is my body; and in like manner he took the cup, and blessed it, and said, This is my blood"; and he gave it to them alone. The same thing in the mysteries of Mithra, also, the evil demons imitated, and commanded to be done; for bread and a cup of water are placed in the mystic rites for one who is to be initiated, with the addition of certain words, as you know or may learn.

67. But we, after these things, henceforward always remind one another of them; and those of us who have the means assist all who are in want;

and we are always together. And in all our oblations we bless the Maker of all things, through his Son Jesus Christ, and through the Holy Ghost. And on the day which is called Sunday there is an assembly in the same place of all who live in cities or in country districts; and the records of the apostles, or the writings of the prophets, are read as long as we have time. Then the reader concludes, and the president verbally instructs and exhorts us to the imitation of these excellent things. Then we all rise together and offer up our prayers. And, as I said before, when we have concluded our prayer, bread is brought, and wine and water, and the president in like manner offers up prayers and thanksgivings with all his strength, and the people give their assent by saying Amen; and there is a distribution and a partaking by every one of the eucharistic elements, and to those who are not present they are sent by the hands of the deacons. And such as are in prosperous circumstances, and wish to do so, give what they will, each according to his choice; and what is collected is placed in the hands of the president, who assists the orphans, and widows, and such as through sickness or any other cause are in want; and to those who are in bonds, and to strangers from afar, and, in a word, to all who are in need, he is a protector. But Sunday is the day on which we all hold our common assembly, because it is the first day on which God, when he changed the darkness and matter, made the world; and Jesus Christ our Saviour on the same day rose from the dead: for the day before that of Saturn he was crucified, and on the day after it, which is Sunday, he appeared to his apostles and disciples, and taught them these things which we have given to you also for your consideration.

68. If, then, these things appear to you to have reason and truth, respect them; but if they seem

to be frivolous, hold them in contempt as frivolities; and do not decree death against those who have done no wrong, as if they were enemies. For we forewarn you that you shall not escape the future judgment of God, if you continue in your injustice; and we will exclaim, Let what is pleasing to God be done. And although, from the letter of the greatest and most illustrious Emperor Adrian your father, we might entreat you to command that judgment should be done according to our petition, yet it is not on the ground of Adrian's decision that we the rather urged this; but we have made our appeal and exposition, because we know that we ask what is just. I have, however, subjoined a copy of Adrian's letter that you may know that we speak truth in this also. The copy is as follows:

Epistle of Adrian in behalf of the Christians.

I have received the letter addressed to me by your predecessor Serenius Granianus, a most illustrious man; and this communication I am unwilling to pass over in silence, lest innocent persons be disturbed, and occasion be given to the informers for practicing villainy. Accordingly, if the inhabitants of your province will so far sustain this petition of theirs as to accuse the Christians in some court of law, I do not prohibit them from doing so; but I will not suffer them to make use of mere entreaties and outcries. For it is far more just, if any one desires to make an accusation, that you give judgment upon it. If, therefore, any one makes the accusation, and furnishes proof that the said men do anything contrary to the laws, you shall adjudge punishments in proportion to the offenses. And this, by Hercules, you shall give special heed to, that if any man shall, through mere calumny, bring an accusation against any of these persons, you shall award to him more severe punishments in proportion to his wickedness.

SYNOPSIS OF DIALOGUE WITH TRYPHO.

Walking in the Xystus (at Ephesus), Justin is addressed by Trypho, a Jew, who, emboldened by Justin's dress, asks for instruction for himself and friends. J.—"And in what would you be profited by philosophy so much as by your own lawgiver and the prophets?" T.—"Do not the philosophers turn every discourse on God?" Justin replies that, while granting to God a general care of the universe, most philosophers deny his attention to individuals, and so take license for their conduct. Others, claiming that the soul is both immortal and insensible to suffering, teach that it needs nothing from God. Asked for his own opinion, he says that he has studied with the Stoics, the Peripatetics, and the Platonists; that Platonism had seemed most satisfactory to him; but that once, while meditating near the seashore, a venerable man had appeared and, in a learned conversation, shown him the insufficiency of his philosophy, and had then told him of the prophets, who, being filled with the Holy Ghost, had revealed divine truth authoritatively, glorifying the God and Father of all things, and proclaiming his Son, the Christ. The old man had disappeared, "but straightway," says Justin, "a flame was kindled in my soul; and a love of the prophets, and of those men who are friends of Christ, possessed me; and while revolving his words in my mind, I found this philosophy alone to be safe and profitable." Assuring Trypho that he too may find happiness in Christ, the Jew replies that it is better to be circumcised and observe the law. Justin in reply proposes to prove that Christians have not believed empty fables, "but words filled with the Spirit of God and big with power." Some of his companions jeer, but Trypho seats himself respectfully to hear the argument. His opposition to Christians, he says, is simply that they do not observe the law; he does not share the vulgar belief in their immorality.

Justin accordingly begins by declaring that the law is abrogated by the new covenant made in Christ, adducing Scripture to prove that such a new and universal law should succeed. This law the Jews despise, but Isaiah teaches that sin is to be cleansed, not by the blood of sacrifices, but by the blood of Christ (Isa. liii.). Baptism in Christ alone purifies, as says Isaiah, who also describes the true fasting. Circumcision was given to the Jews to designate them for persecution for their treatment of Christ. The Jews, spreading calumnies everywhere against Christians, are responsible both for their own and for others' sins. Christians would observe the law if they did not know why it was given. The patriarchs were acceptable to God without circumcision; thus God, in enjoining sacrifices, and the observance of sabbaths, and the choice of meats, had accommodated himself to an unrighteous nation, but had not made such observances works of righteousness. If there was no need of circumcision before Abraham, or of the keeping of sabbaths, etc., before Moses, there is no need now. But while the old circumcision is obsolete, Christ circumcises all who will.

Those who now say they are sons of Abraham, continues Justin, are represented by Isaiah as crying out to God for an inheritance. To this remark Trypho rejoins, "What is this you say? that none of us shall inherit anything in the holy mountain of God?" J.—"I do not say so, but those who persecute Christ, if they do not repent, shall not inherit." Gentiles who believe shall inherit along with patriarchs and prophets and the just descendants of Jacob (Isa. lxii. and lxiii.). T.—" Why do you quote whatever you wish from the prophetic writings, but do not refer to those which command the observance of sabbaths? For Isaiah thus speaks: (Isa. lxviii. 13, 14). J.—The prophets did command like things with Moses, but only from the hardness of the peoples' hearts. Circumcision of the flesh avails nothing to Egyptians; but even Scythians having knowledge of Christ have a circumcision that avails. Those baptized of the Holy Ghost need no other rite.

Christians, says Justin, call upon God through Christ, at whose name demons are now overcome, and whose power at his advent in glory shall be incomparable (Dan. vii. 7–28). Trypho objects that Daniel describes Christ as glorious. Justin distinguishes two advents, one humble, one glorious, quoting Ps. cx. and lxxii., which, he argues, do not refer to Hezekiah and Solomon.

Trypho says that some who confess Jesus eat meat offered to idols. Justin replies that the existence of heretics confirms the prophecy of Christ concerning false apostles coming in his name. He also proves that Christ is called Lord of hosts and should be worshiped. The Jews hate Christians, because these truths convict them of hardness of heart.

Trypho, allowing that Christ must suffer, calls for proof of his identity with Jesus. Justin first alludes to certain figures, and then instances Jesus's birth from a virgin.

To questions Justin replies that those who kept the law before Christ were saved thereby; but not so those who now keep the law. Still, in his opinion, men are at liberty, if they so desire, to keep the law, though some say otherwise.

Resuming the argument, Justin says that Jesus may be proved the Christ without proving that he preëxisted as God, as indeed some (the Ebionites) hold. To the suggestion that Elijah must precede the Christ, Justin says he will in person precede the second coming; but that his spirit, in the person of John, had heralded the first coming. That John was Christ's precursor is shown from Isaiah. Jacob and Zechariah predicted that Christ should ride upon an ass. The "blood of the grape," meaning the blood of Christ, proves that he was not begotten of man, since the blood of the vine is from God.

Trypho asks that any God but God the Father may, without metaphor, be shown him from Scripture. Justin proves that God who appeared to Abraham is distinguished from God the Father; also God who appeared to Jacob and to Moses. He then adduces the "Wisdom" begotten of the Father, and the words, "Let us make man." Trypho admits the proof, but says he does not need Christ. Justin, adducing further proof, explains the passage, "my glory will I not give to another." He proves that Christ was born of a virgin, whereupon Trypho compares him with Perseus. Justin convicts him of bad faith, and shows how the devil had invented fables about Bacchus, Hercules, and Æsculapius; also that the mysteries of Mithras are distorted from prophecies. The Jews have cut out and misinterpreted passages of the version of the Septuagint. The name of God is shown from Exodus to be Jesus (Joshua), and the prophecy of Isaiah is shown to accord with Christ alone. Justin asserts, against Trypho, that the wicked angels revolted against God; and also maintains (saying, however, that some Christians do not) that Jerusalem will be rebuilt, and the saints shall reign there a thousand years, arguing this from Isaiah and the Apocalypse. The prophetical gifts of the Jews were transferred to Christians. After proving further that Jesus is Christ the Lord, and enumerating various Old Testament figures of the wood of the cross, Justin explains the words " The Spirit of God shall rest on him," showing that Christ did not receive the Spirit on account of poverty. He notices the prefigurement of the cross of Christ in Scripture, and holds that the same kind of righteousness has always been taught, and is summed up in two precepts of Christ. Christ upon the cross took upon himself the curse due to us. He then examines Ps. xxii. at length, showing its reference to Christ. The resurrection of Christ also is typified in the history of Jonah. Micah's prediction of the conversion of the Gentiles is already in part fulfilled, and will be entirely fulfilled at the second advent. These two advents were symbolized by the two goats. Continuing, Justin adduces various symbols of the blood of Christ. Joshua, he says, is a figure of Christ. He claims that Zechariah's prediction suits Christians, and speaks of Malachi's prophecy concerning sacrifices. Christians are the holy people promised to Abraham, Isaac, Jacob, and Judah. The belief of the Gentiles in Jesus proves him the Christ. Christians are the true Israel, the sons of God. He further explains the word Israel, and shows the various Old Testament names of Christ, who appeared as a person. Returning to the conversion of the Gentiles, he shows them to be more faithful than the Jews. He notices the power of Jesus's name in the Old Testament. The Jews are hard-hearted; nevertheless Christians pray for them. Leah was a type of the Jewish people, Rachel of the Christian church; Christ serves for both. The Jews, rejecting Christ, had rejected God. Justin exhorts his hearers to be converted. He shows Noah to have been a figure of Christ. In Christ all are free ; but the Jews hope in vain for salvation. The

Jews are not excusable for crucifying Christ, as all men are free agents.

The conference thus ending, the Jews thank Justin and depart.

NOTICE OF THE MURATORIAN FRAGMENT.

THE earliest approach to a Scripture canon or list of the books of Scripture now extant is found in a celebrated Latin manuscript, discovered in the last century by Muratori, at the Ambrosian Library in Milan. This manuscript originally belonged to Columban's monastery at Bobbio, and dates from the seventh or the eighth century. The work is but a fragment, which begins in the midst of a sentence—the sentence following referring to Luke's Gospel—and ends abruptly. There is strong internal evidence that it was translated from the Greek, though some dissent from this view. Its authorship is unknown; but Muratori conjectured that it was by Caius of Rome, and Bunsen has confidently ascribed it to Hegesippus. Most scholars agree that it belongs to the second century, probably not later than A. D. 170, as is apparent from its reference to Pius of Rome as to a contemporary. A later date has been assigned by some, among them Donaldson, but their reasons are not conclusive.

Westcott judges the work to have been apologetical rather than historical, as it omits to refer to books which were certainly received at Rome in the last quarter of the century; or that possibly it is a compilation of passages from a larger work.

The text is very imperfect, the reading in some passages being only conjectural. The translation here given has been amended by the text given in Westcott "On the Canon."

THE MURATORIAN FRAGMENT.

. . . . at which he was present, and so he placed it. The third book of the Gospel according to Luke. Luke, that physician, after the ascension of Christ, when Paul had taken him along with him as a companion of his travels [or, "when Paul had taken him as assistant, since he was desirous of righteousness"], wrote it in his own name, as seemed good to him—notwithstanding he had not himself seen the Lord in the flesh—and according as he was able to understand the same: so he began to speak from the nativity of John. The fourth Gospel is that of John, one of the disciples. When his fellow disciples and overseers urged him, he said, "Fast ye together for me to-day for three days, and let us relate to each other the revelation which we receive." The same night it was revealed to Andrew, one of the apostles, that, while all looked over, John should write out all things in his own name. . . . And therefore, although various beginnings are presented by each book of the gospels, this makes no difference as respects the faith of believers, since all things in all are declared by the one guiding Spirit concerning the nativity, concerning the passion, concerning the resurrection, concerning his intercourse with his disciples, and concerning his two advents—the first, which has been despised in its humility; the second, which is to be distinguished by regal power. . . . What wonder is it, then, that John should address each thing so uniformly in his epistles, saying, in regard to himself, "The things which we have seen with our eyes, and heard with our ears, and our hands have handled, these are the things which we have written"? For he professes himself not only a seer, but also a hearer and also a writer of all the wonderful works of the Lord in order. Now the Acts of all the Apostles were written in one book. Luke embraced in his work to the most excellent Theophilus only the things which were done in his presence; and this is plainly proved by his omission of all mention of the death of Peter and of the setting out of Paul from the city to Spain. . . . Then come the letters of Paul. The letters themselves declare to those who wish to know from what place or from what cause they were sent. First of all there was the letter to the Corinthians forbidding the schism of heresy; then that to the Galatians forbidding circumcision; and then he wrote more largely to the Romans, penetrating into the order of the Scriptures, and showing that Christ is the foundation of them, concerning each of which things we need to speak particularly; since the blessed apostle Paul himself, following the order of his predecessor John, writes only to seven churches by name in the following order: first to the Corinthians, second to the Ephesians, third to the Philippians, fourth to the Colossians, fifth to the Galatians, sixth to the Thessalonians, seventh to the Romans. But to the Corinthians and Thessalonians, though for rebuke he wrote twice, notwithstanding it is known that there is only one Church scattered over the whole earth; and John also, although in the Apocalypse he writes to seven churches, yet speaks to all. Moreover, one was dedicated to Philemon, and one to Titus, and two to Timothy, in consideration of his love and affection for them, yet also in honor of the catholic church and the order of the Church discipline. There is one also in circulation addressed to the Laodiceans, and one to the Alexandrians forged in the name of Paul, bearing upon the heresy of Marcion, and many others which can not be received by the catholic church; for it does not suit to mix vinegar with honey. The letter of Judas also and the two letters of John above-mentioned are reckoned genuine in the catholic church. Also the Wisdom written by the friends of Solomon in his honor. We receive only the revelations of John and Peter, the latter of which some of our people do not wish to be read in the Church. Moreover, Hermas very lately in our times wrote the Pastor in the city of Rome, while his brother Pius sat as overseer in the chair of the church of the city of Rome; and it ought therefore indeed to be read, but it can never be publicly used in the Church, either among the prophets (the number being complete?) or among the apostles. Nor do we receive anything at all of Arsinous, or Valentinus, or Miltiades, who also wrote a new book of psalms for Marcion, along with Basilides, the Asiatic founder of the Cataphrygians.

MELITO.

MELITO, bishop of Sardis, was born early in the century, and lived until after A. D. 169. He claims our attention on account of his voluminous writings, the titles of which indicate to us the subjects engaging the thought of the Christians of his day.

His apology, already noticed, has been preserved to us in a Syriac translation. He also, as a Syriac translation of a list of his works tells us, wrote the following treatises: "On Easter two, and On Polity and On the Prophets; and another On the Church and another On the First Day of the Week; and again another On the Faith of Man; and another On his Formation; and again another On the Hearing of the Ear of Faith; and besides these, On the Soul and Body; and again On Baptism, and On the Truth, and On the Faith; and On the Birth of Christ, and On the Word of his Prophecy; and again On the Soul and on the Body; and another On the Love of Strangers, and On Satan, and On the Revelation of John; and again another On God who put on the Body." To this list Eusebius adds "The Key," of which it is claimed that we have a version in Latin. Excepting this work and the apology, we have only fragments of Melito's writings. One of these fragments, however, thought to belong to the work On Faith, is of great interest as furnishing an approach to a confession of faith of the church of that day.

EXTRACT FROM MELITO'S WORK ON FAITH.

We have made collections from the law and the prophets relating to those things which are declared concerning our Lord Jesus Christ, that we might prove to your love that he is the perfect Reason, the Word of God; who was begotten before the light; who was Creator together with the Father; who was the Fashioner of man; who was all things in all; who among the patriarchs was Patriarch; who in the law was Law; among the priests, Chief Priest; among kings, Governor; among the prophets, Prophet; among the angels, Archangel; among voices, the Word; among spirits, Spirit; in the Father, the Son; in God, God, the King for ever and ever. For this is he who was Pilot to Noah; who conducted Abraham; who was bound with Isaac; who was in exile with Jacob; who was sold with Joseph; who was Captain with Moses; who was the Divider of the inheritance with Jesus the son of Nun; who in David and the prophets foretold his own sufferings; who was incarnate in the Virgin; who was born at Bethlehem; who was wrapped in swaddling-clothes in the manger; who was seen of the shepherds; who was glorified of the angels; who was worshiped by the Magi; who was pointed out by John; who assembled the apostles; who preached the kingdom; who healed the maimed; who gave light to the blind; who raised the dead; who appeared in the temple; who was not believed on by the people; who was betrayed by Judas; who was laid hold on by the priests; who was condemned by Pilate; who was pierced in the flesh; who was hanged upon the tree; who was buried in the earth; who rose from the dead; who appeared to the apostles; who ascended into heaven; who sitteth on the right hand of the Father; who is the Rest of those who are departed, the Recoverer of those who are lost, the Light of those who are in darkness, the Deliverer of those who are captives, the Guide of those who have gone astray, the Refuge of the afflicted, the Bridegroom of the Church, the Charioteer of the cherubim, the Captain of the angels, God who is of God, the Son who is of the Father, Jesus Christ, the King for ever and ever. Amen.

ATHENAGORAS.

ALTHOUGH Athenagoras was the superior of all in his own age, in literary merit and in broad philosophic culture, we yet know but little of his life. One of our sources of information—the writings of Philip of Sida, who tells us that Athenagoras was the leader of the school at Alexandria in the reign of Hadrian and Antoninus—is not trustworthy. The only other source is the following inscription on the manuscripts of Athenagoras's "Apology": "The Embassy of Athenagoras the Athenian, a philosopher and a Christian, to the Emperors Marcus Aurelius Antoninus and Lucius Aurelius Commodus, Armeniaci, Sarmatici, and, what is greatest, philosophers." From this inscription, and from certain internal evidences, this "Embassy" is assigned to the close of A. D. 176 or the beginning of 177. Some think the work to have differed from the ordinary *apology* of that age in that, in the interval of peace in 177, Athenagoras actually went to Rome as a representative of the Christians, and in person presented his arguments before the emperor. The studied compliments of the address favor this supposition, and, as the only event in Athenagoras's life which can be traced even with probability, his admirers naturally fix upon it. Apart from this conjecture we only know that our author was an Athenian and a philosopher, and that he flourished in the reign of Marcus Aurelius.

Besides his scholarly apology—the best defense of the Christians in that age—we have a treatise by him "On the Resurrection of the Dead." The thought of this work shows careful reflection, and is stated with philosophical precision. Scarcely a superfluous word is used, says Donaldson, while the language is beautiful and at times forcible. The treatise is thought to have been delivered before a company of philosophic friends. The arguments adduced are not from Scripture, but such as would emanate from a Christian *philosopher*. A noticeable feature of both treatises is their free reference to and use of the poets and philosophers. The latter are asserted to have mostly believed in the unity of God.

There are numerous manuscripts, of which the three most ancient and most valuable, dating from the tenth and thirteenth centuries, contain both the treatises.

The chapters here given have been corrected according to Professor Gildersleeve's text.

CHAPTERS FROM THE EMBASSY ABOUT CHRISTIANS, BY ATHENAGORAS THE ATHENIAN: PHILOSOPHER AND CHRISTIAN.

To the Emperors Marcus Aurelius Antoninus and Lucius Aurelius Commodus, conquerors of Armenia and Sarmatia, and more than all philosophers.

Chapter 5.—Poets and philosophers have not

been voted atheists for inquiring concerning God. Euripides, speaking of those who, according to popular preconception, are ignorantly called gods, says doubtingly:

> "If Zeus indeed does reign in heaven above,
> Not ever on one man should ills be sent."

But speaking of him who is apprehended by the understanding according to knowledge, as mind has it, he gives his opinion decidedly, thus:

> "Seest thou on high him who, with humid arms,
> Clasps both the boundless ether and the earth?
> Him reckon Zeus, and him regard as God."

For as to these (so-called gods) he neither saw any real existence, to which a name is usually assigned, underlying them ("Zeus," for instance: "who Zeus is I know not, but by report"), nor that any names were given to realities which actually do exist (for of what use are names to those who have no real existences underlying them?) But him [he did see] by means of his works, considering with an eye to things unseen the things which are manifest in air, in ether, on earth. Him, therefore, from whom proceed all created things, and by whose Spirit they are governed, he concluded to be God; and Sophocles agrees with him when he says:

> "There is one God, in truth there is but one,
> Who made the heavens, and the broad earth beneath."

[Euripides is speaking] of the nature of God, which fills his works with beauty, and teaching both where God must be, and that he must be One.

Chapter 6.—Philolaus, too, when he says that all things are included in God as in a stronghold, teaches that he is one, and that he is superior to matter. Lysis and Opsimus—the one defines God as an ineffable number, the other as the excess of the greatest number beyond that which comes nearest to it. So then, since ten is the greatest number according to the Pythagoreans, being the Tetractys, and containing all the arithmetical and harmonic principles, and the nine stands next to it, God is a unit—that is, one. For the greatest number exceeds the next least by one. Then there are Plato and Aristotle—not that I am about to go through all that the philosophers have said about God, as if I wished to exhibit a complete summary of their opinions; for I know that, as you excel all men in intelligence and in the power of your rule, in the same proportion do you surpass them all in an accurate acquaintance with all learning, cultivating as you do each several branch with more success than even those who have devoted themselves exclusively to any one. But, inasmuch as it is impossible to demonstrate without the citations of names that we are not alone in confining the notion of God to unity, I have directed my attention to dogmas. Plato, then, says: "To find out the Maker and Father of this universe is difficult; and when found it is impossible to declare him to all," conceiving of one uncreated and eternal God. And if he recognizes others as well, such as the sun, moon, and stars, yet he recognizes them as created: "gods, offspring of gods, of whom I am the Maker, and the Father of works which are indissoluble apart from my will; but whatever is compounded can be dissolved." If, therefore, Plato is not an atheist for conceiving of an uncreated God, the Framer of the universe, neither are we atheists who acknowledge and firmly hold that he is God who has framed all things by the Logos, and holds them in being by his Spirit. Aristotle, again, and his followers, recognizing the existence of one whom they regard as a sort of compound living being, speak of God as consisting of soul and body, thinking his body to be the ethereal space and the planetary stars and the sphere of the fixed stars, moving in circles; but his soul, the reason which presides over the motions of the body, itself not subject to motion, but becoming the cause of motion to the other. The Stoics also, although by the appellations they employ to suit the changes of matter, which they say is permeated by the Spirit of God, they multiply the Deity in name, yet in reality they consider God to be one. For, if God is an artistic fire advancing methodically to the production of [the several things in] the world, embracing in himself all the seminal principles by which each thing is produced in accordance with fate, and if his Spirit pervades the whole world, then God is one according to them, being named Zeus in respect of the fervid part of matter, and Hera in respect of the air, and called by other names in respect of that particular part of matter which he pervades.

Chapter 10.—That we are not atheists, therefore, seeing that we acknowledge one God, uncreated, eternal, invisible, impassible, incomprehensible, illimitable, who is apprehended by the understanding only and the reason, who is encompassed by light, and beauty, and spirit, and power ineffable, by whom the universe has been created through his Logos, and set in order, and is kept in being— I have sufficiently demonstrated. [I say "his Logos"], for we acknowledge also a Son of God. Nor let any one think it ridiculous that God should have a Son. For we do not think concerning God the Father or concerning the Son, with the poets who fictitiously represent the gods as no better than men. But the Son of God is the Logos of the Father, in idea and in energy; for after the pattern of him and by him were all things made, the Father and the Son being one. And, the Son being in the Father and the Father in the Son, in oneness and power of spirit, the understanding and reason of the Father is the Son of God. But if, in your surpassing intelligence, it occurs to you to inquire what is meant by the Son, I will state briefly that he is the first product of the Father, not as having been brought into existence (for from the beginning God, who is the eternal mind, had the Logos in himself, being from eternity instinct with Logos); but in that he came forth to be the idea and energizing power of all material things, which lay like a nature without attributes, and an inactive earth, the grosser particles being mixed up with the lighter. The prophetic Spirit also agrees with our statements. "The Lord," it says, "made me the beginning of his ways to his works." The Holy Spirit himself also, which operates in the prophets, we assert to be an effluence of God, flowing from him, and returning back again like a beam of the sun. Who, then, would not be astonished to hear men who speak of God the Father, and of God the Son, and of the Holy Spirit, and who declare both their power in union and their distinction in order, called atheists? Nor is our teaching in what relates to the divine nature confined to these points; but we recognize also a multitude of angels and ministers, whom God the Maker and Framer of the world distributed and appointed to their several posts by his Logos, to occupy themselves about the elements, and the heavens, and the world and the things in it, and the goodly ordering of them all.

Chapter 13.—But, as most of those who charge us with atheism, and that because they have not even the dreamiest conception of what God is, and are doltish and utterly unacquainted with natural and divine things, and such as measure piety by the rule of sacrifices, charge us with not acknowledging the same gods as the cities, be pleased to attend to the following considerations, O Emperors, on both points. And first, as to our not sacrificing: The Framer and Father of this universe does not need blood, nor the odor of burnt-offerings, nor the fragrance of flowers and incense, forasmuch as he is himself perfect fragrance, needing nothing either within or without; but the noblest sacrifice to him is for us to know who stretched out and vaulted the heavens, and fixed the earth in its place like a center; who gathered the water into seas, and divided the light from the darkness; who adorned the sky with stars, and made the earth to bring forth seed of every kind; who made animals and fashioned man. When, holding God to be this Framer of all things, who preserves them in being and superintends them all by knowledge and administrative skill, we "lift up holy hands" to him, what need has he further of a hecatomb?

> " For they, when mortals have transgressed or failed
>   To do aright, by sacrifice and prayer,
>   Libations and burnt offerings, may be soothed."

And what have I to do with hecatombs, which God does not stand in need of?—though indeed it does behoove us to offer a bloodless sacrifice and "the service of our reason."

Chapter 16.—Beautiful without doubt is the world, excelling as well in its magnitude as in the arrangement of its parts, both those in the oblique circle and those about the north, and also in its spherical form. Yet it is not this, but its Artificer, that we must worship. For when any of your subjects come to you, they do not neglect to pay their homage to you, their rulers and lords, from whom they will obtain whatever they need, and address themselves to the magnificence of your palace; but if they chance to come upon the royal residence, they bestow a passing glance of admiration on its beautiful structure: but it is to you yourselves that they show honor, as being "all in all." You sovereigns, indeed, adorn your palaces for yourselves; but the world was not created because God needed it; for God is himself everything to himself—light unapproachable, a perfect world, spirit, power, reason. If, therefore, the world is an instrument in tune, and moving in well-measured time, I adore the Being who gave its harmony, and strikes its notes, and sings the accordant strain, and not the instrument; for at the musical contests the adjudicators do not pass by the lute-players and crown the lutes. Whether then, as Plato says, the world be a product of divine art, I admire its beauty and adore the Artificer; or whether it be his essence and body, as the Peripatetics affirm, we do not neglect to adore God, who is the cause of the motion of the body, and descend "to the beggarly and weak elements," adoring in the impassible air (as they term it) passible matter; or, if any one apprehends the several parts of the world to be powers of God, we do not approach and do homage to the powers, but their Maker and Lord. I do not ask of matter what it has not to give, nor, passing God by, do I pay homage to the elements which can do nothing more than what they were bidden; for, although they are beautiful to look upon, by reason of the art of their Framer, yet they still have the nature of matter. And to this view Plato also bears testimony; "for," says he, "that which is called heaven and earth has received many blessings from the Father, but yet partakes of body; hence it can not possibly be free from change." If, therefore, while I admire the heavens and the elements in respect of their art, I do not worship them as gods, knowing that the law of dissolution is upon them, how can I call those objects gods of whom I know the makers to be men?

Chapter 25.—These angels, then, who have fallen from heaven, and haunt the air and the earth, and are no longer able to rise to heavenly things, and the souls of the giants, which are the demons who wander about the world, perform actions, the demons such as resemble the natures they have received, the angels such as accord with the appetites they have indulged. But the prince of matter, as may be seen merely from what transpires, exercises a control and management contrary to the good that is in God:

> "Ofttimes this anxious thought has crossed my mind,
> Whether 'tis chance or deity that rules
> The small affairs of men, and, spite of hope
> As well as justice, drives to exile some
> Stripped of all means of life, while others still
> Continue to enjoy prosperity."

Prosperity and adversity, contrary to hope and justice, made it impossible for Euripides to say to whom belongs the administration of earthly affairs, which is of such a kind that one might say of it:

> "How then, while seeing these things, can we say
> There is a race of gods, or yield to laws?"

The same thing led Aristotle to say that the things below the heavens are not under the care of Providence, although the eternal providence of God concerns itself equally with us below—

> "The earth, let willingness move her or not,
> Must herbs produce, and thus sustain my flocks "—

and addresses itself to the deserving individually, according to truth and not according to opinion; and all other things, according to the general constitution of nature, are provided for by the law of reason. But because the demoniac movements and operations proceeding from the adverse spirit produce these disorderly sallies, and moreover move men, some in one way and some in another, as individuals and as nations, separately and in common, in accordance with the tendency of matter on the one hand, and of the affinity for divine things on the other, from within and from without, some who are of no mean reputation have therefore thought that this universe is constituted without any definite order, and is driven hither and thither by an irrational chance; not understanding that of those things which belong to the constitution of the whole world, there is nothing out of order or neglected, but that each one of them has been produced by reason, and that therefore they do not transgress the order prescribed to them; and that man himself, too, so far as he that made him is concerned, is well ordered, both by his original nature, which has one common character for all, and by the constitution of his body, which does not transgress the law imposed upon it, and by the termination of his life, which remains equal and common to all alike; but that, according to the character peculiar to himself and the operation of the ruling prince and of the demons his followers, he is impelled and moved in this direction or in that, notwithstanding that all possess in common the same original constitution of mind.

THE TREATISE OF ATHENAGORAS ON THE RESURRECTION OF THE DEAD.

Closing Argument.

Each of those things which are constituted by nature, and of those which are made by art, must have an end peculiar to itself, as indeed is taught us by the common sense of all men, and testified by the things that pass before our eyes. For do we not see that husbandmen have one end, and physicians another, and again the things which spring out of the earth another, and the animals nourished upon it, and produced according to a certain natural series, another? If this is evident, and natural and artificial powers, and the actions arising from these, must by all means be accompanied by an end in accordance with nature, it is absolutely necessary that the end of men, since it is that of a peculiar nature, should be separated from community with the rest; for it is not lawful to suppose the same end for beings destitute of rational judgment, and of those whose actions are regulated by the innate law and reason, and who live an intelligent life and observe justice. Freedom from pain, therefore, can not be the proper end for the latter, for this they would have in common with beings utterly devoid of sensibility: nor can it consist in the enjoyment of things which nourish or delight the body, or in an abundance of pleasures; else a life like that of the brutes must hold the first place, while that regulated by virtue is without a final cause. For such an end as this, I suppose, belongs to beasts and cattle, not to men possessed of an immortal soul and rational judgment.

Nor again is it the happiness of soul separated from body: for we are not inquiring about the life or final cause of either of the parts of which man consists, but of the being who is composed of both; for such is every man who has a share in this present existence, and there must be some appropriate end proposed for this life. But if it is the end of both parts together, and this can be discovered neither while they are living in the present state of existence through the numerous causes already mentioned, nor yet when the soul is in a state of separation, because the man can not be said to exist when the body is dissolved, and indeed entirely scattered abroad, even though the soul continue by itself, it is absolutely necessary that the end of man's being should appear in some reconstitution of the two together, and of the same living being. And as this follows of necessity, there must by all means be a resurrection of the bodies which are dead, or even entirely dissolved, and the same men must be formed anew; since the law of nature ordains the end not absolutely, nor as the end of any men whatsoever, but of the same men who passed through the previous life; but it is impossible for the same men to be reconstituted unless the same bodies are restored to the same souls. But that the same soul should obtain the same body is impossible in any other way, and possible only by the resurrection; for if this takes place, an end befitting the nature of men follows also. And we shall make no mistake in saying, that the final cause of an intelligent life and rational judgment is, to be occupied uninterruptedly with those objects to which the natural reason is chiefly and primarily adapted, and to delight unceasingly in the contemplation of *Him who is*, and of his decrees; notwithstanding that the majority of men, because they are affected too passionately and too violently by things below, pass through life without attaining this object. For the large number of those who fail of the end that belongs to them does not make void the common lot, since the examination relates to individuals, and the reward or punishment of lives ill or well spent is proportioned to the merit of each.

THE END.

EARLY CHRISTIAN LITERATURE PRIMERS.

EDITED BY
Professor GEORGE PARK FISHER, D. D.

The "Early Christian Literature Primers" will embody, in a few small and inexpensive volumes, the substance of the characteristic works of the great Fathers of the Church. The plan recognizes four groups of works:

1. *The Apostolic Fathers, and the Apologists*, A. D. 95–180.
2. *The Fathers of the Third Century*, A. D. 180–325.
3. *The Post-Nicene Greek Fathers*, A. D. 325–750.
4. *The Post-Nicene Latin Fathers*, A. D. 325–590.

These groups are to be embraced in four books. In the first book are given exact translations of the principal works of the Apostolic Fathers and the Apologists, preceded by introductions upon the writings of the period, and by sketches of the several authors. Nearly every known author of the period is mentioned, and his place pointed out. Only genuine works, as translated from the latest critical texts, have been admitted, and of these a very large part have been brought in.

BY REV. GEORGE A. JACKSON.

THE APOSTOLIC FATHERS, and the APOLOGISTS.

A. D. 95–180.

CONTENTS: Introduction — The Earlier Patristic Writings — THE APOSTOLIC FATHERS—Clement of Rome—Sketch, Epistle to Corinthians, and Clementine Literature; Ignatius—Sketch, and Epistle to Romans, Ephesians, and Polycarp; Polycarp—Sketch, and Epistle to Philippians; Barnabas—Sketch, and Epistle. Associated Authors. Hermas—Sketch, and the Shepherd; Papias—Sketch, and Fragments.

THE APOLOGISTS.—Introductory Sketch—Notice, and Epistle to Diognetus; Justin—Sketch, First Apology, and Synopsis of Dialogue with Trypho; Author of Muratorian Fragment, and the Fragment; Melito—Sketch, and Fragment; Athenagoras—Sketch, Chapters from Mission about Christians, and Final Argument on the Resurrection.

[NOW READY.]

D. APPLETON & CO., PUBLISHERS, NEW YORK.

EARLY CHRISTIAN LITERATURE PRIMERS.

EDITED BY

Professor GEORGE PARK FISHER, D.D.

IN PREPARATION:

THE FATHERS OF THE THIRD CENTURY.

CONTENTS: Introduction (A. D. 180–325), on the Influence of Origen in the East and of Cyprian in the West—Irenæus—Hippolytus—Clement of Alexandria—Origen—Methodius—Tertullian—Cyprian.

THE POST-NICENE GREEK FATHERS.

CONTENTS: Introduction (A. D. 325–750), on the Schools of Alexandria and Antioch—Eusebius of Cæsarea—Athanasius—Basil—Gregory of Nyssa—Gregory Nazianzen—Epiphanius—John Chrysostom—Theodore of Mopsuestia—Theodoret—Cyril of Alexandria—The Historians of the Fifth and Sixth Centuries.

THE POST-NICENE LATIN FATHERS.

CONTENTS: Introduction (A. D. 325–590), on the Influence of the Roman Jurisprudence upon the Latin Church Writers—Lactantius; Hilary; Ambrose; Jerome; Augustine; John Cassian; Leo the Great; Gregory the Great; the Historians Rufinus, Sulpicius Severus, and Cassiodorus.

D. APPLETON & CO., PUBLISHERS, NEW YORK.

ART PUBLICATIONS.

American Painters:

Eighty-three Engravings from Pictures by Native Artists. 4to. Cloth, $7.00; morocco, $13.00.

The Turner Gallery.

A Series of One Hundred and Twenty Engravings on Steel, from the Works of J. M. W. TURNER, R. A. In two folio volumes. Published by subscription. Half morocco, $32.00; full morocco, $36.00.

The Poet and Painter;

OR, GEMS OF ART AND SONG. Containing Selections from the English Poets. Illustrated with 99 Steel Engravings printed on the page with the text. New edition. Imperial 8vo. Cloth, extra, $12.00; morocco, $20.00.

Studio, Field, and Gallery.

A Manual of Painting for the Student and Amateur, with Information for the General Reader. By HORACE J. ROLLIN. 12mo. Cloth, $1.50.

Pottery and Porcelain,

From Early Times down to the Philadelphia Exhibition of 1876. By CHARLES WYLLYS ELLIOTT. With 165 Illustrations, and the more Important Marks and Monograms. 1 vol., small 4to. Cloth, gilt, $5.00; morocco, $10.00.

Bibelots and Curios.

A Manual for Collectors. With a Glossary of Technical Terms. By FRÉDÉRIC VORS. 16mo, cloth. Price, 75 cents.

Schools and Masters of Painting,

With an Appendix on the Principal Galleries of Europe. By A. G. RADCLIFFE. Illustrated. Cloth, $3.00; half morocco, $5.00.

The Art Journal:

An International Gallery of Engravings by Distinguished Artists of Europe and America, with Illustrated Papers in the Various Branches of Art. Price, 75 cents per Number; $9.00 per Annum.

D. APPLETON & CO., PUBLISHERS, 549 & 551 BROADWAY, N. Y.

CLASSICAL WRITERS.

Edited by JOHN RICHARD GREEN.

16mo. Flexible cloth. . . *Price,* 50 *cents.*

UNDER the above title, Messrs. D. APPLETON & Co. are issuing a series of small volumes upon some of the principal Classical and English writers, whose works form subjects of study in our colleges, or which are read by the general public concerned in Classical and English literature for its own sake. As the object of the series is educational, care is taken to impart information in a systematic and thorough way, while an intelligent interest in the writers and their works is sought to be aroused by a clear and attractive style of treatment. Classical authors especially have too long been regarded as mere instruments for teaching pupils the principles of grammar and language, while the personality of the men themselves, and the circumstances under which they wrote, have been kept in the background. Against such an irrational and one-sided method of education the present series is a protest.

It is a principle of the series that, by careful selection of authors, the best scholars in each department shall have the opportunity of speaking directly to students and readers, each on the subject which he has made his own.

The following volumes are in preparation:

GREEK.

HERODOTUS..............Professor BRYCE.
SOPHOCLES..............Professor LEWIS CAMPBELL.
DEMOSTHENES..........S. H. BUTCHER, M. A.
EURIPIDES..............Professor MAHAFFY. [*Ready.*

LATIN.

VIRGIL..................Professor NETTLESHIP.
HORACE................T. H. WARD, M. A.
CICERO.................Professor A. S. WILKINS.
LIVY....................W. W. CAPES, M. A.

ENGLISH.

MILTON................Rev. STOPFORD BROOKE.
                                        [*Ready.*
BACON.................Rev. Dr. ABBOTT.
SPENSER...............Professor J. W. HALES.
CHAUCER...............F. J. FURNIVALL.

Other volumes to follow.

D. APPLETON & CO., NEW YORK.

RECENT
EDUCATIONAL WORKS.

Words,
And how to put them together. By HARLAN H. BALLARD, Principal of Lenox High-School, Lenox, Mass. 18mo. Cloth, 40 cents.

General History,
From B. C. 800 to A. D. 1876. Outlined in Diagrams and Tables; with Index and Genealogies. For General Reference, and for Schools and Colleges. By SAMUEL WILLARD, A. M., M. D., Professor of History in Chicago High-School. 8vo. Cloth, $2.00.

Principles and Practice of Teaching.
By JAMES JOHONNOT. 12mo. Cloth, $1.50.

Harkness's Preparatory Course in Latin Prose Authors.
Comprising four books of Cæsar's Gallic War, Sallust's Catiline, and eight Orations of Cicero. With Notes, Illustrations, a Map of Gaul, and a Special Dictionary. 12mo. Cloth, $1.75.

Harkness's Sallust's Catiline.
With Notes and a Special Vocabulary. 12mo Cloth, $1.15.

The Latin Speaker.
Easy Dialogues, and other Selections for Memorizing and Declaiming in the Latin Language. By FRANK SEWALL, A.M. 12mo. Cloth, $1.00.

Appletons' School Readers.
By WILLIAM T. HARRIS, A. M., LL. D., Superintendent of Schools, St. Louis, Mo.; ANDREW J. RICKOFF, A. M., Superintendent of Instruction, Cleveland, Ohio; and MARK BAILEY, Instructor in Elocution, Yale College.

Appletons' First Reader................Price, 25 cents.
Appletons' Second Reader............ " 40 "
Appletons' Third Reader.............. " 52 "
Appletons' Fourth Reader............. " 70 "
Appletons' Fifth Reader................ $1.25 "

D. APPLETON & CO., PUBLISHERS, 549 & 551 BROADWAY, NEW YORK

RECENT EDUCATIONAL WORKS.—(Continued.)

Education as a Science.

By ALEXANDER BAIN, LL. D., Professor of Logic in the University of Aberdeen. (Forming Vol. XXV. of "The International Scientific Series.") 12mo. Cloth, $1.75.

A Hand-book of Requirements for Admission to the Colleges of the United States,

With Miscellaneous Addenda, for the Use of High-Schools, Academies, and other College Preparatory Institutions. Compiled and arranged by A. F. NIGHTINGALE, A. M. Large 8vo. Cloth. Price, $1.00.

Elementary Lessons in Historical English Grammar,

Containing Accidence and Word Formation. By the Rev. RICHARD MORRIS, LL. D., President of the Philological Society, London. 18mo. Cloth, 254 pages. Price, $1.00.

Primer of the Natural Resources of the United States.

By J. HARRIS PATTON, author of the "Concise History of the United States." 16mo. Cloth. Uniform with "Science Primers." Price, 45 cents.

The Fairy-Land of Science.

By ARABELLA B. BUCKLEY, author of "A Short History of Natural Science," etc. With numerous Illustrations. 1 vol., 12mo, 244 pages. Cloth, price, $1.50.

The Study of Rocks.

An Elementary Text-Book in Petrology. With Illustrations. By FRANK RUTLY, of the English Geological Survey. Forming a new volume in "Text-Books of Science Series." 16mo. Cloth. 819 pages. Price, $1.75.

For sale by all booksellers. Any volume mailed, post-paid, to any address in the United States, on receipt of price.

D. APPLETON & CO., PUBLISHERS, 549 & 551 BROADWAY, NEW YORK.

APPLETONS' SCHOOL READERS,

CONSISTING OF FIVE BOOKS.

BY

WM. T. HARRIS, LL. D.,
Superintendent of Schools, St. Louis, Mo.

A. J. RICKOFF, A. M.,
Superintendent of Instruction, Cleveland, O.

MARK BAILEY, A. M.,
Instructor in Elocution, Yale College.

	RETAIL PRICES.
APPLETONS' FIRST READER.............	$0 25
APPLETONS' SECOND READER..........	40
APPLETONS' THIRD READER............	52
APPLETONS' FOURTH READER..........	70
APPLETONS' FIFTH READER.............	1 25

CHIEF MERITS.

These Readers, while avoiding extremes and one-sided tendencies, combine into one harmonious whole the several results desirable to be attained in a series of school reading-books. These include good pictorial illustrations, a combination of the word and phonic methods, careful grading, drill on the peculiar combinations of letters that represent vowel-sounds, correct spelling, exercises well arranged for the pupil's preparation by himself (so that he shall learn the great lessons of self-help, self-dependence, the habit of application), exercises that develop a practical command of correct forms of expression, good literary taste, close critical power of thought, and ability to interpret the entire meaning of the language of others.

THE AUTHORS.

The high rank which the authors have attained in the educational field and their long and successful experience in practical school-work especially fit them for the preparation of text-books that will embody all the best elements of modern educative ideas. In the schools of St. Louis and Cleveland, over which two of them have long presided, the subject of reading has received more than usual attention, and with results that have established for them a wide reputation for superior elocutionary discipline and accomplishments. Feeling the need of a series of reading-books harmonizing in all respects with the modes of instruction growing out of their long tentative work, they have carefully prepared these volumes in the belief that the special features enumerated will commend them to practical teachers everywhere.

Of Professor Bailey, Instructor of Elocution in Yale College, it is needless to speak, for he is known throughout the Union as being without a peer in his profession. *His methods make natural, not mechanical readers.*

D. APPLETON & CO., 549 & 551 *Broadway, New York.*

PRIMERS
IN SCIENCE, HISTORY, AND LITERATURE.

18mo. . . . . Flexible cloth, 45 cents each.

I.—Edited by Professors HUXLEY, ROSCOE, and BALFOUR STEWART.

SCIENCE PRIMERS.

Chemistry......H. E. ROSCOE.
Physics...BALFOUR STEWART.
Physical Geography....A. GEIKIE.
Geology............A. GEIKIE.
Physiology.......M. FOSTER.
Astronomy...J. N. LOCKYER.
Botany..........J. D. HOOKER.
Logic............W. S. JEVONS.
Inventional Geometry, W. G. SPENCER.
Pianoforte.........FRANKLIN TAYLOR.
Political Economy....W. S. JEVONS.

II.—Edited by J. R. GREEN, M. A., *Examiner in the School of Modern History at Oxford.*

HISTORY PRIMERS.

Greece............C. A. FYFFE.
Rome..........M. CREIGHTON.
Europe.........E. A. FREEMAN.
Old Greek Life.........J. P. MAHAFFY.
Roman Antiquities...A. S. WILKINS.
Geography...GEORGE GROVE.

III.—Edited by J. R. GREEN, M. A.

LITERATURE PRIMERS.

English Grammar........R. MORRIS.
English Literature....STOPFORD BROOKE.
Philology............J. PEILE.
Classical Geography....M. F. TOZER.
Shakespeare....E. DOWDEN.
Studies in Bryant, J. ALDEN.
Greek Literature, R. C. JEBB.
English Grammar Exercises, R. MORRIS.
Homer......W. E. GLADSTONE.

(Others in preparation.)

The object of these primers is to convey information in such a manner as to make it both intelligible and interesting to very young pupils, and so to discipline their minds as to incline them to more systematic after-studies. They are not only an aid to the pupil, but to the teacher, lightening the task of each by an agreeable, easy, and natural method of instruction. In the Science Series some simple experiments have been devised, leading up to the chief truths of each science. By this means the pupil's interest is excited, and the memory is impressed so as to retain without difficulty the facts brought under observation. The woodcuts which illustrate these primers serve the same purpose, embellishing and explaining the text at the same time.

D. APPLETON & CO., 549 & 551 *Broadway, New York.*

HISTORY OF OPINIONS
ON THE
SCRIPTURAL DOCTRINE OF RETRIBUTION.
By EDWARD BEECHER, D. D.,
Author of "The Conflict of Ages."

1 vol., 12mo. - - - - - - Cloth, $1.25.

The momentous question of future retribution is here historically discussed with an earnestness and deliberation due to its transcendent importance. The main interest of the inquiry naturally centers in the doom of the wicked. Will it be annihilation? ultimate restoration to holiness and happiness? endless punishment? or is it out of our power to decide which of these views is the truth? The discussion is intensified by being narrowed to the meaning of a single word, *aionios*. The opinions of those to whom Christ spoke, and how they understood him, are vital questions in the argument; and, to solve them, the opinions and modes of speech of preceding ages must be attentively weighed, for each age is known to have molded the opinions and use of words of its successor. Hence, Dr. Beecher has found himself compelled to "trace the development of thought and language from the outset to the days of Christ, then to inquire into the import of his words, in the light of all preceding ages; and, lastly, to trace the development of opinion downward through the Christian ages."

STUDIES IN THE CREATIVE WEEK.
By Rev. GEORGE D. BOARDMAN, D. D.

1 vol., 12mo. Cloth, $1.25.

The Lectures, fourteen in number, embrace the following topics: 1. INTRODUCTION; 2. GENESIS OF THE UNIVERSE; 3. OF ORDER; 4. OF LIGHT; 5. OF THE SKY; 6. OF THE LANDS; 7. OF PLANTS; 8. OF THE LUMINARIES; 9. OF ANIMALS; 10. OF MAN; 11. OF EDEN; 12. OF WOMEN; 13. OF THE SABBATH; 14. PALINGENESIS.

"We see in the Lectures more than the sensation of the hour. They will have a marked effect in defining the position of the believer of to-day, in certifying both to disciple and to skeptic just what is to be held against all attack; and the statement of the case will be in many cases the strongest argument. They will tend to broaden the minds of believers, and to lift them above the letter to the plane of the spirit. They will show that truth and religion are capable of being defended without violence, without denunciation, without misrepresentation, without the impugning of motives."—*National Baptist*.

"Revelation and Science can not really conflict, because 'truth can not be contrary to truth;' but so persistent have been the attacks of scientists on time-honored orthodoxy, that the believer in Revelation has long demanded an exhaustive work on the first chapter of Genesis. In response to this widespread feeling, the Rev. George Dana Boardman, D. D., the learned pastor of the First Baptist Church, Philadelphia, was requested to deliver a course of lectures covering this debatable ground."

D. APPLETON & CO., PUBLISHERS, 549 & 551 BROADWAY, N. Y.

THE LIFE AND WORDS OF CHRIST.

By CUNNINGHAM GEIKIE, D. D.

With Twelve Engravings on Steel. In Two Volumes, 8vo. Price. $8.00.

"A work of the highest rank, breathing the spirit of true faith in Christ."—*Dr. Delitzsch, the Commentator.*

"A most valuable addition to sacred literature."—*A. N. Littlejohn, D. D., Bishop of Long Island.*

"I have never seen any life of our Lord which approached so near my ideal of such a work."—*Austin Phelps, D. D., author of " The Still Hour,"* etc.

"A great and noble work, rich in information, eloquent and scholarly in style, earnestly devout in feeling."—*London Literary World.*

"Without disparaging in any sense the noble labors of his predecessors, we think Dr. Geikie has caught a *new ray* from the 'Mountain of Light,' and has added a new page to our Christology which many will delight to read. These volumes are full of exquisite word-painting, from which an artist might reproduce innumerable life-like pictures."—*Evangelist.*

TENT-WORK IN PALESTINE.

A RECORD OF DISCOVERY AND ADVENTURE.

By CLAUDE REIGNIER CONDER, R. E.,

Officer in Command of the Survey Expedition. Published for the Committee of the Palestine Exploration Fund.

With Thirty-three Illustrations by J. W. Whymper.

Two vols., 8vo. Cloth, $6.00.

"The account of Lieutenant Conder's labors is not merely the interesting record of a great work, it has the additional charm of being exceedingly well written; and it will always remain one of the most valuable contributions to the literature on Palestine."—*Pall Mall Gazette.*

THE EPISTLE TO THE HEBREWS;

With Notes, Critical, Explanatory, and Practical.

By the Rev. HENRY COWLES, D. D.,

Author of "The Minor Prophets," "Ezekiel and Daniel," "The Revelation of John," "Hebrew History," etc.

1 vol., 12mo. Cloth. Price, $1.50.

D. APPLETON & CO., Publishers, 549 & 551 Broadway, N. Y.

THE BOOK OF JOB:

ESSAYS, AND A METRICAL PARAPHRASE.

By ROSSITER W. RAYMOND, Ph. D.

With an Introductory Note by the Rev. T. J. Conant, D. D.

12mo. - - - Cloth, $1.25.

"The book is in iambic tetrameter rhyming verse, with three-lined stanzas. Of course it does not follow the original word for word, though it keeps remarkably close to the literal translation; and where it departs from the literal it often brings out the meaning of the original more clearly than a word-for-word rendering can do. But as a reproduction of the spirit and tone of the original, as a translation—a carrying over—into English, not of its words and phrases, but of the poem as a whole, the writer has done with his paraphrase what it would be perhaps impossible to do in a literal translation. Regarded merely as an attempt to create on the mind of the English reader something of the impression which the Hebrew poem made on the minds of those to whom it was first rehearsed, Mr. Raymond's paraphrase is perhaps the best English translation of Job that has yet been made. The rendering is printed in parallel columns with Conant's translation, and is accompanied with copious introduction and notes."—*N. Y. Independent.*

THE COMPREHENSIVE CHURCH;

OR,

Christian Unity and Ecclesiastical Union in the Protestant Episcopal Church.

By the Right Rev. THOMAS H. VAIL, D. D., LL. D., Bishop of Kansas.

12mo. - - - Cloth, $1.25.

"As far as it goes it is the best book of the kind we have ever seen, and it goes far enough, considering the object which the author had in view. It is just the thing to put into the hands of those who are ignorant concerning the principles and customs of the Church. A general and hearty welcome, we are sure, awaits it."—*N. Y. Churchman.*

"An able and excellent teacher of the true position of the Church."—*N. Y. Episcopal Register.*

"Bishop Vail presents his views with an impressive sincerity, which will not only commend the volume to those who share his belief, but also to all thoughtful readers."—*Providence Journal.*

D. APPLETON & CO., Publishers, 549 & 551 Broadway, N. Y.

www.ingramcontent.com/pod-product-compliance
Lightning Source LLC
Chambersburg PA
CBHW020826230426
43666CB00007B/1112